The Film Industry

Navigating the World of Film and Filmmaking. Part-2

ELIO E

 ElioEndless

ELIO ENDLESS PUBLISHERS

For more information or to book an event, please contact: elioendleeshouse@gmail.com

Book design by Kai

Cover design by Tyson

Paperback ISBN:

ebook ISBN:

To Dad, Mom, and my supportive colleagues,Your love, guidance, and unwavering support have been the driving force behind my journey as a writer. Thank you for believing in me and encouraging me to pursue my dreams. Your presence in my life has made all the difference.

With heartfelt gratitude,

ELIO.E

Preface

Hey there, "wave"! How's it going? I'm your friendly neighborhood book editor, here to tell you about this amazing book that just landed on our shelves. It's a gem that our awesome publishing company has brought to life. Now, as part of my job, I get to dive into countless books, and I must say, this one is an absolute delight. No need for any unnecessary delay, let me give you a sneak peek into what makes it so worthwhile. Are you ready? Let's jump right in with the introduction.Before venturing into the enthralling world of film, one must first get familiar with the fundamental notion of a movie genre, which is an essential thematic and artistic categorization that guides one through the complicated web of filmmaking. This nuanced categorization not only delineates the creative essence of a cinematic piece, but it also assists cinephiles and academics in comprehending the core elements that define each genre, which can range from the enthralling exploits of adventure to the imaginative wonders of science fiction on the big screen.An creative endeavor that is carefully created to provoke certain feelings, tell singular storylines, and resound with a variety of audiences, each film genre is analogous to a different brushstroke on the canvas of cinema. The show Adventure, for example, goes on a journey that is full of daring exploits, exciting adventures, and unknown territory. It captivates viewers with an adrenaline-filled journey that fires the spirit of exploration and discovery.The genre of fantasy, on the other hand, unfolds a world that is filled with entrancing marvels, magical worlds, and mythical beings. This transports viewers to a realm that is beyond the ordinary, where the borders of reality disintegrate, and dreams come to life via the medium of a hypnotic narrative tapestry. It is a genre that celebrates the use of imagination and encourages the audience to suspend their disbelief so that they may become engrossed in a world that is replete with enchantment and whimsy.As it delves farther, the field of science fiction explores undiscovered regions of the future, putting scientific plausibility in contrast with imaginative creativity. It pushes the boundaries of human comprehension and mulls over the 'what ifs' of technological developments, space travel, and the existence of life beyond Earth. Exploration of the human potential—reflecting our anxieties, hopes, and moral conundrums in the context of a technologically advanced society—is at the heart of science fiction. This is the genre's defining characteristic.In addition, the fabric of film extends into the realm of drama, which is characterized by complex human feelings and plots that are intended to compel the audience's attention. The art of drama involves the weaving of elaborate stories that delve into the complexities of human relationships, the workings of society, and the ups and downs of an individual's life. It elicits self-reflection and, as a result of its unfiltered honesty and powerful emotional resonance, it leaves an unforgettable impact on the viewer's psyche.Romance, a subgenre of storytelling that is nearly as ancient as the art form itself, captivates audience members' emotions and transports them into the warm embrace of love. It evokes a spectrum of emotions that extend beyond the screen and echo inside the depths of the human soul by weaving storylines of passion, heartbreak, and the triumph of devotion.Fear and adrenaline surges are elicited by the genre of horror, which is characterized by spine-chilling plots and frightening atmospheres. It appeals to our most basic drives and worst phobias, challenging us to face the macabre and the supernatural while delving into the dark shadows that lie in the corners of our mind.In essence, the wide variety of film genres spans a vast panorama of narrative, with each conveying a tale in a unique way that is distinctive in its aim, structure, and emotional impact. Aficionados and cinephiles alike will find that gaining an appreciation for the various facets of cinematic creativity is made easier by developing an awareness of the subtleties of the various film genres. This will result in a more profound connection and an enhanced viewing experience. Therefore, as the trip through film continues, let us enjoy the kaleidoscope diversity of genres, each of which is a brushstroke adding to the brilliant mosaic that is the world of cinema.

Acknowledgements

I would like to take this opportunity to extend my heartfelt thanks to all the individuals who have played a significant role in the creation of this non-fiction book. Your unwavering support, valuable advice, and constant encouragement have been invaluable throughout this journey. I am deeply grateful to those who have provided me with aspirational direction, constructive criticism, and kind advice. Your feedback has been instrumental in shaping the content and direction of this book. I genuinely appreciate your candid insights into my project.I am particularly grateful for the exceptional assistance of Mr. Jaffer and Mrs. Sameena at Endless Publishers. Their continuous support, dedication, and guidance have been instrumental in helping me overcome obstacles and improve the quality of my work. I am sincerely appreciative of their tremendous efforts and unwavering belief in this project.I would also like to express my heartfelt appreciation to Mr. Ahmed, my project's external advisor from Ahmed Corporation. His invaluable advice, insightful critique, and vast wisdom have played a pivotal role in refining my thoughts and enhancing the overall quality of this book. I am truly grateful for his guidance and expertise.Furthermore, I would like to acknowledge Ms. Sultana and every individual who has contributed to obtaining the necessary resources and making this initiative possible. Your assistance, whether it was in sourcing information, conducting research, or providing logistical support, is deeply appreciated. This book would not have come to fruition without your invaluable contributions.I cannot overlook the individual who initially sparked the flame of inspiration within me to embark on this book-writing endeavor. Your unwavering belief in my abilities, continuous motivation, and unending support throughout this artistic process have been instrumental in my journey. I am forever indebted to you for being my constant source of inspiration.I want to express my deepest gratitude to every person who has contributed to this project, no matter how small their role may have been. Each and every one of you has played a part in making this book possible, and your contributions have not gone unnoticed. Your support, encouragement, and assistance have been instrumental in bringing this book to fruition.Finally, I would like to give special credit to Kai, B.EE, and Tyson, the pen names that have accompanied me on this writing adventure. Your creativity, distinct perspectives, and unique insights have added depth and character to this book. I am honored to have had the opportunity to collaborate with you.To all of you who have been a part of this remarkable journey, I extend my deepest gratitude. Your unwavering support, guidance, and friendship have been invaluable. Thank you for believing in me and for contributing to the realization of this non-fiction book.With

sincere appreciation,
Elio Endless

EDITOR NOTE

1. Publisher Notes: This edition is a product of inspiration from other works, with a portion of its content derived from public domain sources. Elioendless, the creator, editor, and publisher of the ebook edition, utilized manuscripts, select texts, and illustrative images from public domain archives. Members can acquire this ebook from our website for personal use. However, please note that any form of commercial storage, transmission, or reverse engineering of this file is strictly prohibited.

Contents

CHAPTER ONE

Film Genres and Styles

Overview of major film genres (e.g., drama, comedy, action, sci-fi)

Before venturing into the enthralling world of film, one must first get familiar with the fundamental notion of a movie genre, which is an essential thematic and artistic categorization that guides one through the complicated web of filmmaking. This nuanced categorization not only delineates the creative essence of a cinematic piece, but it also assists cinephiles and academics in comprehending the core elements that define each genre, which can range from the enthralling exploits of adventure to the imaginative wonders of science fiction on the big screen.

An creative endeavor that is carefully created to provoke certain feelings, tell singular storylines, and resound with a variety of audiences, each film genre is analogous to a different brushstroke on the canvas of cinema. The show Adventure, for example, goes on a journey that is full of daring exploits, exciting adventures, and unknown territory. It captivates viewers with an adrenaline-filled journey that fires the spirit of exploration and discovery.

The genre of fantasy, on the other hand, unfolds a world that is filled with entrancing marvels, magical worlds, and mythical beings. This transports viewers to a realm that is beyond the ordinary, where the borders of reality disintegrate, and dreams come to life via the medium of a hypnotic narrative tapestry. It is a genre that celebrates the use of imagination and encourages the audience to suspend their disbelief so that they may become engrossed in a world that is replete with enchantment and whimsy.As it delves farther, the field of science fiction explores undiscovered regions of the future, putting scientific plausibility in contrast with imaginative creativity. It pushes the boundaries of human comprehension and mulls over the 'what ifs' of technological developments, space travel, and the existence of life beyond Earth. Exploration of the human potential—reflecting our anxieties, hopes, and moral conundrums in the context of a technologically advanced society—is at the heart of science fiction. This is the genre's defining characteristic.In addition, the fabric of film extends into the realm of drama, which is characterized by complex human feelings and plots that are intended to compel the audience's attention. The art of drama involves the weaving of elaborate stories that delve into the complexities of human relationships, the workings of society, and the ups and downs of an individual's life. It elicits self-reflection and, as a result of its unfiltered honesty and powerful emotional resonance, it leaves an unforgettable impact on the viewer's psyche.Romance, a subgenre of storytelling that is nearly as ancient as the art form itself, captivates audience members' emotions and transports them into the warm embrace of love. It evokes a spectrum of emotions that extend beyond the screen and echo inside the depths of the human soul by weaving storylines of passion, heartbreak, and the triumph of devotion.Fear and adrenaline surges are elicited by the genre of horror, which is characterized by spine-chilling plots and frightening atmospheres. It appeals to our most basic drives and worst phobias, challenging us to face the macabre and the supernatural while delving into the dark shadows that lie in the corners of our mind.In essence, the wide variety of film genres spans a vast panorama of narrative, with each conveying a tale in a unique way that is distinctive in its aim, structure, and emotional impact. Aficionados and cinephiles alike will find that gaining an appreciation for the various facets of cinematic creativity is made easier by developing an awareness of the subtleties of the various film genres. This will result in a more profound connection and an enhanced viewing experience. Therefore, as the trip through film continues, let us enjoy the kaleidoscope diversity of genres, each of which is a brushstroke adding to the brilliant mosaic that is the world of cinema.

What Are Movie Genres?

Film genres function as the primary classification systems, enabling films to be arranged into subcategories according to narrative and aesthetic characteristics. Not only do these subgenres provide a sneak peek into the narrative and aesthetic of a film, but they also play a significant part in the development of the film's characters, places, plot structures, and overall tonal characteristics.

When we dig into the varied world of film genres, we are exposed to a wide range of different cinematic experiences. Films in the action genre, for example, are defined by sequences that are guaranteed to get your heart racing, and they frequently use slow-motion images that increase the impact of critical situations. The storyline of a horror film depends on tense moments, which are usually punctuated by jump scares. This creates an environment where action takes precedence over lengthy discussion.The panorama of cinema genres includes main categories such as action, adventure, comedy, drama, fantasy, horror, musicals, mystery, romance, science fiction, sports, thriller, and Western. Other primary classifications include science fiction, sports, and thriller. Each genre has its own distinctive taste, which allows it to appeal to a diverse range of audience preferences. Musicals captivate viewers by incorporating song and dance into the narrative in a way that is not distracting from the action on screen, whereas action flicks take them on exciting excursions.In addition, several genres have a scope that goes beyond their core classification because they incorporate concepts that cut across multiple categories. Films about war, for example, frequently combine aspects of action, drama, and suspense in order to depict the brutal reality of armed warfare. In a similar fashion, zombie movies combine aspects of horror and thriller, delving into the world of the undead while simultaneously keeping spectators on the edge of their seats.In a nutshell, film genres play an essential part in the development of the cinematic environment. They provide a window into the heart of a movie and direct the anticipations of moviegoers, all of which contribute to the creation of an experience that is both varied and satisfying when they go to the movies.

Comedy Genre

Comedy movies are a subgenre of motion pictures that are known for their ability to stimulate our sense of humor and make us laugh till we can't stop smiling and crying with joy. These cinematic masterpieces are predicated on a comic concept, which often involves placing a character in a predicament that is either hard, funny, or just plain ridiculous, and in which they are hilariously ill-equipped to handle. Not only does a good comedy movie's genius reside in its unrelenting bombardment of laughs, but also in its skillful presentation of a globally accessible, real-life tale that is inhabited with people as complicated as a labyrinth, each of whom is starting on a path of growth and enlightenment. This is what makes a good comedy movie brilliant.

Within the large field of comedy, the myriad of subgenres that exist provide depth and diversity, therefore expressing a wide range of humorous nuances. A mockumentary, which is a satirical representation of real-life events with a comedic spin, provides an insightful look into the oddities of human behavior thanks to its one-of-a-kind perspective. Dark comedy, often known as black comedy, is a kind of comedy that digs into the gloomy and macabre, deftly finding humorous moments in the most depressing aspects of life. A fan-favorite genre, the romantic comedy combines the ups and downs of romantic relationships with a sprinkling of witty banter to create a story that makes audiences laugh till their tummies hurt and their hearts race.Parody and spoof are forms of humor that brilliantly mock established genres, tropes, or cultural phenomena. They call to those who take pleasure in sarcasm and humorous exaggeration. The slapstick comedy is a time-honored classic that honors the art of physical humor and antics that are overdone. It elicits laughter through the sheer absurdity of the actions and situations that are depicted in the comedy."The Jerk" (1979), in which the great Steve Martin plays the lead role of the film's protagonist, is widely regarded as one of the most prestigious gems in the comedy film collection. The story revolves on a man who has an uncanny lack of rhythm and discernment. He finds himself accidentally absorbed into a Black family of sharecroppers, and it is only then that he realizes his incongruous whiteness. The movie presents a picture of hilarious escapades and cultural misunderstandings, and it serves as an important reminder that comedy transcends the borders of race and culture, bringing all of us together in laughing.

Drama Genre

The drama genre is the epitome of narratives that are marked by elevated stakes and a myriad of conflicts, constructing elaborate tales that pivot around the development of a primary storyline. Dramatic stories are often told in the form of films, television shows, and plays. This type of storytelling calls for an extremely thorough orchestration, as well as the requirement that each character and scene actively move the plot along with purpose and meaning. Within the sphere of drama, adherence to a rigorously established narrative framework is of the utmost importance. This allows for the representation of real-life circumstances or the delving into the depths of severe situations to be carried out in a seamless manner. These depictions include characters who are emotionally charged, with each of their actions and reactions being tightly woven into the fabric of the narrative.

The investigation of the range of human experiences and feelings is given even more breadth and depth by drama's many subgenres. Both historical drama and costume drama have the ability to take viewers to bygone centuries and immerse them in a world that is imbued with the spirit of those eras. Romantic drama dives into the depths of love and relationships, illuminating the intricate workings of the human heart in the process. The ups and downs of adolescence, together with the intense feelings that come with this stage of life, are well captured in the genre of television known as teen drama. The high-stakes world of healthcare is examined in medical drama, which frequently delves into the personal lives of both medical workers and the patients they treat to illustrate the stark contrast between life and death. Docudrama is a hybrid medium that combines documentary and dramatic storytelling to show actual events in an engaging and attention-grabbing way. On the other side, the cinema noir and neo-noir subgenres delve into the murkier aspects of human existence, probing the darker parts of society as well as the human mind.Iconic motion pictures serve as foundations of aesthetic and narrative quality throughout this vast canvas of dramatic story telling. The representation of ambition, power, and the human need for a legacy that is found in the 1941 film "Citizen Kane" captivates moviegoers. The subtleties of organized crime, power relationships, and familial devotion are all explored in "The Godfather" (1972), which paints a colorful tapestry of human impulses. The film "The Social Network" from 2010 expertly navigates the digital era and the beginnings of a social network empire, depicting themes of ambition, friendship, and betrayal against the backdrop of technical advancement. These motion pictures not only embody the dramatic genre but also go beyond the confines of the subgenre, leaving an unforgettable stamp on the landscape of film.

Action Genre

Action movies are notorious for moving at a breakneck speed and including a number of exciting sequences. These sequences can include dramatic fight scenes, high-speed chases, and fascinating slow-motion images. One may see a wide variety of characters, ranging from awe-inspiring superheroes to highly talented martial artists, all engaged in daring and thrilling acts under this genre. Not only does the progression of the story make up the core of action movies, but so does the precise execution of these heart-pounding, adrenaline-fueled moments that leave audiences poised on the tip of their seats and anxiously expecting the next spectacular sequence.

The genre of action movies covers a wide range of topics and can take place in a variety of environments. The canvas of action movies is expansive and densely detailed, ranging from gritty cop dramas that dig into the seedy underbelly of law enforcement to catastrophic catastrophe flicks that display mankind struggling with immediate threat, and even include spy storylines that are packed with intrigue and espionage. These films cover a wide range of subject matter."True Lies," a cinematic masterpiece directed by James Cameron and released in 1994, is widely regarded as a prime example of this subgenre. The film tells the narrative of an American spy, who is played by the legendary Arnold Schwarzenegger. The movie embodies the very essence of action by merging a captivating story with heart-stopping action sequences in a way that is seamless, and as a result, it has captured the imagination of people all over the world.It is very necessary for anyone who aspires to write their own high-octane storylines within this exhilarating genre to familiarize themselves with the skill of crafting action screenplays. The nuances of writing a compelling action screenplay that keeps spectators on the edge of their seats and wanting more may be understood by aspiring screenwriters with the help of our thorough guide, which provides insights that are of immeasurable value.

Science Fiction Genre

The ability of science fiction to create vast and wondrous landscapes is one of its most defining characteristics. It is recognized for portraying parallel realities that are alive with inventive features that go beyond the confines of the reality we are familiar with. This subgenre encompasses a wide range of subject investigations, frequently digging into topics like as time travel and space exploration while imagining events that will take place in the far future. The stories that are contained under this category all deal with the effects and implications that are a direct result of the constantly shifting landscape of technology and scientific developments.

When it comes to the genre of science fiction movies, the craft of world-building is given painstaking attention and consideration. Every precise detail, from the layout of faraway cities to the workings of futuristic technology, has been painstakingly designed in order to give the impression that the viewer should have no trouble believing what they are seeing. This meticulous attention to detail is absolutely necessary in order to guarantee that the audience is completely submerged in the narrative and the vast universe that it takes place inside.In the field of cinematic arts, notable examples of science fiction include the legendary "Star Wars" film, which was released in 1977 and took spectators to a galaxy far, far away while also unraveling a narrative of epic proportions. The remarkable effect that the 1999 film "The Matrix" had on viewers was the result of its clever investigation of the intricate relationship between reality and synthetic existence. In addition, the film "Inception," which was released in 2010, went into the inner workings of the human mind, investigating the complexities of dreams and awareness, so securing its position as an exemplary work of science fiction cinema. These movies are great examples of the inventive power that the genre is known for. They have the ability to captivate spectators with their innovative narratives and push the limits of what is possible.

Genre-generating Factors and Historical Changes

The idea of literary genres is a fluid and complex one that is shaped by a wide variety of circumstances, including societal standards, cultural environment, ideological limitations, technical demands, and the qualities of the audience for whom the writing is meant. These elements, which are sometimes grouped together and referred to as genre-generating characteristics, play an essential part in determining the shape that a literary work could become.

The precise situation that is now taking place usually influences the genre that the author chooses to write in. For example, a novel probably isn't the best choice for addressing a congregation, and a poem probably doesn't have the kind of depth that's required to adequately describe the complexity of a civil war. In a similar vein, the cultural register of the audience has a significant influence on the decision that the writer makes. The expectations of nobles are vastly different from those of townsfolk, which leads to the selection of genres such as odes or humorous mock hymns that are suited for the audience.

It is arguable that one of the most significant aspects that generates genres is the social and educational status of the audience, which in turn shapes the historical supremacy of specific literary forms over different eras. An example of this would be the English Renaissance, particularly during the Elizabethan period, which is commonly referred to as the "Golden Age" of English drama. The most prominent form of artistic expression during this time period was drama, and one of the most significant figures of that age, William Shakespeare, was particularly successful in this field. Although he is most known for his dramatic works, he also made significant contributions to the fields of poetry and sonnet writing.Inevitably, a literary genre will not acquire supremacy in a particular historical time unless a number of criteria are met that are just right. On the other hand, the absence of specific requirements might serve as a factor in the generation of a genre. For example, during Shakespeare's time period, the prevalent social conditions were not favorable to the development of novels or tales since they discouraged reading. The vast bulk of the population was incapable of reading or writing, literary organizations were in their formative phases, and monetary restraints made purchasing books difficult. Therefore, the most prevalent type of entertainment was drama, which could be witnessed in its raw, uncut form at well-known theaters.As the centuries passed, so did the landscape of literary supremacy. With the advent of a new genre, the novel, which mirrored the rising of the middle class, often known as the English bourgeoisie, the landscape of literary dominance changed. This literate and socially involved bourgeoisie was the driving force behind the demand for novels, which handled contemporary social and political concerns. As a result, the novel became the preeminent form of literary expression.When one follows the history of British literature, one discovers that the supremacy of different literary genres and the structures of those genres are subject to a consistent ebb and flow that is intimately related to the predominate cultural tastes of each century. Each era gave rise to unique tendencies toward certain genres, beginning with the religiously dominated Middle Ages and continuing on through the experimental Renaissance and the spectacle-rich Restoration. Romanticism disrupted traditional genre boundaries by promoting imagination and embracing a range of subjects. This tendency continued into the 20th century with high modernism and postmodernism, questioning and blurring conventional genre classifications. Romanticism demolished established genre boundaries by advocating imagination and embracing a variety of themes.

In reaction to changes in society, philosophical ideas, and aesthetic movements, literary genres have consistently morphed, interwoven, and developed over the course of the history of literature. During the Victorian era, for instance, there was a rise in the popularity of the book, which provided an in-depth investigation of the human psychology as well as societal traditions and morals. The rigidity of genre borders, however, began to erode as the 20th century progressed, notably during the era of high modernism, and later on into the age of postmodernism, as the weight of experimentation and invention began to bear down on them.

High modernism, which emerged in the early 20th century, marked a break from traditional narrative forms. It presented readers with a variety of challenges, including fragmented frameworks, various points of view, and sometimes ambiguous interpretations. This literary movement was exemplified by prominent authors such as Virginia Woolf and James Joyce, who rejected traditional methods of narrative in favor of a more subjective and introspective method of approaching writing. These authors are considered to have been the pioneers of the modernist literary movement.Pos tmodernism is a literary and creative movement that emerged in the middle of the 20th century. It is distinguished by a skepticism toward big narratives, an acceptance of pastiche and metafiction, and a blurring of barriers between high and low culture. Thomas Pynchon and Salman Rushdie are two authors who are known for experimenting with the norms of multiple genres by weaving aspects from a variety of genres together to create narratives that are difficult to classify.The impact of postmodernism has only grown stronger over the past few decades. The advent of the digital age and the widespread availability of the internet have broadened the creative frontiers available to authors, making it possible for them to experiment with new forms of storytelling such as multimedia storytelling, hypertext tales, and interactive fiction. As a result of the increased fluidity and hybridization of genres, writers frequently draw aspects from a variety of genres in order to create distinctive literary experiences.In the world of modern literature, the demarcation of literary genres has grown even more intricate as a result of the fact that authors frequently resist conventional classifications. There has been a rise in the popularity of works that combine elements from two different genres, such as fantasy and romance or history and science fiction. This is a reflection of the changing interests and preferences of a broad readership. As we go ahead into a future that is unpredictable, the trajectory of literary genres will continue to be an open-ended story. This is because the trajectory of literary genres is continuously altered by the interaction of societal upheavals, technology breakthroughs, and the inventive inventiveness of writers. It is possible that the lines dividing literary genres will continue to blur, which will result in the development of a diverse literary expression that resists simple categorization and encourages readers to investigate the ever-expanding worlds of their own imagination.

The Art of Storytelling in Film, An Exploration of the styles of storytelling.

Within the field of cinematic creativity, the concept of "film storytelling" refers to the sophisticated process of utilizing both audible and visual components in order to successfully communicate a captivating story or narrative to an audience that is attracted by it. This complex process involves a careful interplay of speech, characters, scenes, music, and special effects, all of which must be arranged harmoniously to produce a narrative that is consistent and captivating.

The progression of the story is accomplished through the medium of film by combining sounds and images in fascinating ways. The visual aspects compose the canvas, furnishing the setting and the surrounding environment for the story as it develops, while the aural components contribute additional layers of information and emotional resonance. This story is amplified by the strategic use of lighting, a variety of camera angles, and other forms of visual creativity, which helps to produce particular moods and atmospheres.

When it comes to the art of presenting stories through the medium of cinema, the primary purpose is to create a narrative that is captivating and immersive, one that both captivates the audience and emotionally resonates with them. When a film's narrative is well-crafted, it has the ability to transport viewers and make them feel as though they are an important part of the developing plot. This impression stays with viewers long after the film's titles have rolled.It is of the utmost significance to recognize that the art of narrative in film is of the utmost importance in the art of filmmaking, serving as the cornerstone of any project involving the moving image. It is the very heart of the matter, the center of everything, and the element that is fundamentally the most important for maintaining audience interest. A film's ability to tell a narrative well may make all the difference in its level of success, while telling a tale that is badly conceived can invariably lead to the film's failure. But within this art form, there is a profusion of a wide variety of narrative styles and approaches, each of which contributes to the enrichment of the cinematic environment. In this section, we go deeper into the world of the expository style, which is a popular and often used technique.When narrating a story in an expository manner, the teller adopts a more instructive tone and presents facts, information, or background elements that are necessary for the audience to understand the story. This mode is analogous to peeling back the layers of a story, gradually exposing the fundamental components that underpin the action that is taking place in the narrative. It frequently acts as a channel for enlightenment for the audience, ensuring that there is clarity and a thorough knowledge of the events as they develop.In the form of storytelling known as expository storytelling, filmmakers use a variety of strategies to elaborate on significant elements. This may be speech that is unambiguous and straightforward, which communicates vital information, or the employment of narrators who lead the audience through the complexities of the plot. In addition, the use of visual aids like flashbacks, montages, or informational graphics may be utilized to strengthen the narrative, which in turn improves the viewer's ability to comprehend the material and enhances the overall viewing experience.In the end, the expository style serves as a beacon of clarity and explication, seeking to guarantee that the viewer grasps the underlying fabric of the story, so increasing their involvement and making their cinematic trip more fulfilling.

Linear:

In a linear narrative, the story is told in a straightforward and well-organized fashion, following to a chronological sequence that reflects the order in which events took place as they were taking place. The audience is provided with a plain and simply consumable structure, which enables them to follow the plot in a logical development, thanks to the narrative technique known as "storytelling." In essence, it adheres to the normal progression of time and events by detailing them in the order in which they took place when they first took place.

Movies like "Forrest Gump" and "The Shawshank Redemption" provide an excellent illustration of this kind of narrative telling through their respective portrayals of the main character. The plot of "Forrest Gump" deftly follows the life of the titular character from his youth to his maturity, catching the events as they occur, one after another, in a manner that is consistent and unbroken over the entirety of the narrative. In a similar manner, "The Shawshank Redemption" makes expert use of this linear narrative style to depict the life of Andy Dufresne as he copes with the difficulties of incarceration. It does so by illustrating the sequence of events in a way that reflects the passage of time and the development of his path toward redemption. The filmmakers are able to convey the tale in a manner that is both logical and intuitive when they adhere to a chronological format, which guarantees that the audience will have no trouble understanding the progression of the plot. This method creates a more consistent and immersive watching experience for the audience, which in turn improves their level of involvement with the narrative as well as their capacity to understand it.

Non-linear:

Within the field of narrative structure, we come across an intriguing method known as the non-linear storytelling method. This approach tells the tale in a way that does not follow a linear progression. This method of storytelling does not follow the typical chronological order. Instead, it chooses to depict the events and developments of the storyline in a way that is deliberately disconnected and temporally fractured. It is an intentional break from the chronological course of a traditional story, with the goal of engaging the audience in a manner that is both one of a kind and thought-provoking.

This nontraditional approach to narrating a tale involves the progression of the story being told in a series of jumps and shifts in time, with flashbacks and flashforwards being utilized frequently. The flow of the tale can be gently shaped by the revelation of significant events from the story's past or by delivering glimpses into the story's future through these narrative jumps, which can be subtle or apparent. The use of such manipulation of time serves to heighten the mystery and intricacy of the tale, entrancing the audience in a mystery-like experience that requires their active participation in order to solve.The critically praised movie "Pulp Fiction" is a great example of this non-linear method of conveying a story, and it does it very effectively. This cinematic masterpiece, which was directed by Quentin Tarantino, skillfully ties together a variety of different tales and presents them in a manner that is non-sequential. A higher degree of cognitive involvement from the audience is required in order for them to piece together the jigsaw that is the storyline as a result of the purposeful fragmentation of the narrative, which not only heightens the sense of mystery but also increases its intensity.This non-linear narrative structure is utilized to great advantage in the film "Memento," which is also considered to be an important cinematic achievement. By depicting the events in the film in the opposite sequence in which they occurred in real life, director Christopher Nolan creates an experience that is like riding a mental rollercoaster. This option was made on purpose, and it not only places the audience inside the head of the protagonist, who has problems with short-term memory, but it also defies the assumptions that are typically associated with narrative.In its most basic form, non-linear storytelling is a demonstration of how the craft of narrative production is continuously developing. As a result of its departure from the conventional, linear progression of time, it provides a new perspective through which we may investigate the interconnectivity of events and the intricacies of the human experience. It forces us to solve the riddle of a story by peeling back its layers in a way that encourages introspection and sparks the imagination, and it does it in a way that is compelling.

Subjective

Storytelling that is expository takes on a point of view that is profoundly ingrained in the viewpoint of a single character. It reveals the tale through tracing the character's thoughts, feelings, and perceptions. By taking this strategy, the viewer is placed into the character's mental space, and the presentation of the tale is molded depending on the characters' individual experiences. The films "Fight Club" and "The Perks of Being a Wallflower" are two well-known examples of the subjective form of narrative that is utilized in these films. In these kinds of movies, the audience is completely submerged in the mind of the main character, which enables them to have a deeper understanding of that character and, as a result, to have a significant impact on the progression of the story as a whole. The filmmakers use this kind of storytelling to cultivate a sense of intimacy and connection between the audience and the character, providing a novel lens through which the audience may view and interact with the events that are taking place in the tale.

Objective:

The events of an expository narrative are told through a lens that is all-seeing and does not focus on a single vantage point. The audience is not limited to a single point of view, as is the case with other narrative approaches; rather, they are provided with the opportunity to observe and grasp the most private thoughts and actions of each and every character. This approach makes it possible to get a bird's-eye view of the plot and sheds light on the objectives, challenges, and victories experienced by each character in the novel.

The movie "The Godfather," which is often considered to be a cinematic classic due to the painstaking detail with which it depicts the dynamics of a strong criminal family, is an example that epitomizes this method. In this movie, the spectator is not restricted to the thoughts of a single character; rather, they are privy to the complex web of intents and acts that define the lives of the characters. Every subtlety, every struggle, and every alliance is exposed, which contributes to developing an all-encompassing comprehension of the intricate underworld that is portrayed.Similarly, "The Social Network" takes on the same kind of explanatory narrative approach as "The Social Network," shedding light on the beginnings and growth of the Facebook empire. The film does not limit itself to the viewpoint of a single individual, which enables a more comprehensive picture of the complex social and technical world that serves as the basis for the story. This approach offers a comprehensive knowledge of the wide cast of personalities and the roles they played within the enthralling chronicle of Facebook's genesis and the following challenges faced by its designers.

Realistic:

The art of expository storytelling is communicating information and presenting facts in a way that is understandable and instructive. When it comes to the world of cinematic storytelling, a realistic story is one that has been carefully designed to reflect the complexities and relationships that exist in real life. Characters, scenes, and events are painstakingly crafted to be credible and to relate with the viewer, providing a feeling of authenticity in the process. This strategy tries to completely submerge viewers in a universe that is reflective of their own life experiences and points of view.

Take into consideration illustrious works of film such as "The Pursuit of Happyness" and "American Beauty," in which the storytellers deftly accept this realistic technique. The storyline of "The Pursuit of Happyness" develops in a way that is reflective of the challenges and victories that a great number of people go through in their efforts to achieve success and happiness in their lives. The realism of the tale as a whole is enhanced by the trials that are endured by the protagonist, the accurate depiction of the circumstances in which he finds himself, and the final triumph over the difficulties that he encounters.In a similar vein, the movie "American Beauty" dives into the nuances of suburbia life and investigates the secret conflicts and aspirations that lie underneath the seemingly commonplace façade of its characters. The characters' complicated lives, their relationships, and the societal constraints they face are shown with a rawness that matches the actual world, shining light on the human condition and society standards in the process of illuminating the human condition.The core of this style rests in its capacity to provide a glimpse into the lives of the characters, so enabling the audience to see the characters' highs and lows, aspirations, and general development throughout the course of the story. It closes the gap between the fictional tale and reality, making it possible for viewers to draw analogies and acquire new insights into the human experience. Filmmakers that use this approach are able to tell tales that have a profound effect on their viewers because they pay painstaking attention to detail and place a strong emphasis on being real.

Surreal:

A surreal story is one that unfolds in the world of narrative expression with an air of the fanciful and dreamy, creating a complex tapestry of the unlikely and the unusual. Characters, places, and events in this strange narrative domain go beyond the bounds of the ordinary, embracing a surreal essence that propels the viewer into a universe that seems to be separated from our own reality. This mysterious way of presenting a narrative, which is comparable to a mirage in the great expanse of imagination, produces a vivid image that transcends the limitations of our worldly experiences.

Imagine a cinematic canvas in which the rules of the everyday kowtow to the caprices of imagination and the everyday is nothing more than a faint reverberation in the background of a huge symphony of the weird. "Inception" and "Eternal Sunshine of the Spotless Mind" are only two examples of the kinds of works that might find a safe haven for their creative development within this narrative dreamscape. The everyday is imbued with an amplified sense of wonder, and the familiar is veiled in a strange cloak in these cinematic masterpieces, which epitomize the art of surreal narrative.In the movie "Inception," we go through the halls of dreams inside dreams, which are places where the very fabric of reality may be changed and remade by the subconscious. As the story progresses, the protagonists traverse a complex narrative while digging further into the mind's layers. As a result, the distinctions between what is real and what is only a product of the imagination become increasingly blurry. The dreamscapes come into view, each one more bizarre than the one before it, demonstrating the inexhaustible capacity of the human imagination.On the other side, "Eternal Sunshine of the Spotless Mind" takes us on an emotional rollercoaster through the shattered memories of a stormy love story. This movie is a masterpiece. The erasure of some memories weaves together the wistful feeling of having lost something with the bizarre idea that one may knowingly change their own history. The narrative dance in this movie is a careful balancing act between the surrealistic manipulation of memory on the one hand, and the profoundly emotional human experiences that resonate through the surrealist lens on the other.The audience is encouraged to suspend their disbelief and fully immerse themselves in the strange paradise that has been constructed by the innovative genius of the storyteller during this wonderful trip of weird storytelling. It is a gateway into the mysterious landscapes of the mind, a place where reality may be twisted and contorted and the bizarre reigns supreme, encouraging us to explore the unknown frontiers of the human imagination.

Episodic:

A narrative that is episodic, as opposed to one that is seamless and continuous, develops through a series of small portions or episodes that are completely separate from one another. This method of writing stories includes deliberately dividing the storyline into several but interrelated sections, with each section having its own distinctive set of thematic themes and character arcs. Films like "Crash" and "Amores perros," which utilize this episodic structure, purposefully use these separate episodes to dig into a variety of story arcs, giving a complex tapestry of experiences and views.

The plot of "Crash" is told through a succession of vignettes that are all related to one another. Each of these vignettes investigates the intricacies of racial and socioeconomic conflicts that exist in modern-day Los Angeles. The film presents viewers with a mosaic of various personalities and circumstances via these vignettes, illustrating the clash of lives and beliefs. A detailed representation of the complexities of human interactions and the workings of society may be achieved via the use of this episodic method, which makes it possible to delve deeply into a variety of different tales.In a similar manner, "Amores perros" adopts an episodic narrative framework in order to weave together numerous stories that are connected by an automobile tragedy. Love, betrayal, and redemption are all depicted amidst the tumultuous metropolitan setting of Mexico City in each of the segments' respective depictions of different individuals and their connected destinies. The use of an episodic approach allows for a more in-depth analysis of relationships as well as the influence that chance occurrences have on those relationships, which contributes to a more all-encompassing picture of the human condition.Both of these movies make use of the episodic storytelling style, which expands the scope of the storyworld, enables a more in-depth investigation of several facets of a topic, and provides an engrossing viewing experience by way of a series of narrative episodes that are fascinating on their own.

Hybrid

It is possible to create a hybrid narrative style by fusing together two or more of the other types of storytelling styles described earlier. This results in a narrative that is more complex and contains a variety of facets. The films "The Big Lebowski" and "The Tree of Life" are two outstanding instances of this one-of-a-kind storytelling approach.

The narrative being told and the audience that the filmmaker has in mind both play a significant role in determining the success of a specific cinematic storytelling technique. There are many distinct ways to tell a tale, and each one has the potential to be effective in varied degrees depending on the type of story being told and the variety of people the teller is trying to captivate.Storytelling that adheres to a linear format, which is defined as an uncomplicated chronological order of events, is successful when used to tales that have a narrative framework that can be understood and followed with relative ease. The audience is able to readily follow the progression of the plot as a result of this. On the other hand, non-linear storytelling shines best in narratives that span numerous complicated storylines. This allows the audience to get varied viewpoints and appreciate the deep relationships between events, which is one of the chief benefits of non-linear storytelling.

Subjective storytelling provides the audience with a fresh perspective through the eyes of a particular character, enveloping them in the emotional and introspective parts of a narrative and drawing their attention to them. On the other hand, objective storytelling functions well in narratives that attempt to be informational and objective, since it provides a glimpse into the thoughts and actions of all of the individuals involved. A personal connection may be fostered between the audience and the people and events that take place inside a story through the use of realistic storytelling, which appeals to stories that strive to be relatable. On the other hand, surreal storytelling incorporates fanciful and dreamy aspects into the story, making it an excellent choice for tales that aim to take the reader or audience beyond the bounds of normal reality. The art of telling stories in bite-sized, manageable chunks or episodes is one of the strengths of the episodic storytelling format. This allows the listener to absorb the narrative in readily consumable portions rather than in a continuous, unbroken flow. On the other hand, hybrid storytelling provides a creative method that is excellent for tales that strive to break away from old conventions. It enables the audience to experience the narrative in a manner that is unrestricted by traditional storytelling rules, which is great for stories that aim to break free from traditional conventions. In the end, the choice of a narrative style need to derive from an in-depth grasp of the tale itself, the audience that the filmmaker has in mind, and the filmmaker's own creative vision. Because of this understanding, it is possible to pick the method of storytelling that is both the most effective and the most compelling, which in turn increases the total impact and resonance of the cinematic experience.

CHAPTER TWO

Film Industry Trends and Innovations

THE ROLE OF VR/AR TECHNOLOGY IN FILM INDUSTRY

The power of a film's narrative to arouse the audience's sympathy and immerse them deeply in the action of the story is one of its most important and distinguishing characteristics. Moving pictures have been used as the principal method for communicating stories throughout the entirety of the film industry's long and illustrious history, which began with rather simple beginnings. This narrative medium developed throughout the course of time, eventually coming to incorporate vibrant colors of color and a symphony of sound, so changing the act of storytelling into an experience that engages many senses. The voyage proceeded along its trajectory, unfolding into the worlds of three-dimensional images, immersive IMAX cinemas, the marvels of computer-generated imagery (CGI), and the beautiful world of animation. Now, at this point in time, we find ourselves at the cusp of a new age, venturing into the unexplored regions of Virtual Reality (VR) and Augmented Reality (AR) in the film industry.

In this day and age of filmmaking, innovators and visionaries are vigorously investigating the possibilities of virtual reality and augmented reality technologies to take the level of immersion to new and uncharted heights. The audience is relegated to the role of mere bystanders in traditional cinematic experiences, regardless of whether the film is presented in 2D or 3D, and must watch the developing action from a distance. The introduction of virtual reality and augmented reality, on the other hand, has signaled a paradigm change, making audiences into active participants rather than only passive viewers. The attractiveness of virtual reality and augmented reality defies conventional bounds, and as a result, it is attracting a wide range of businesses and regions into its fold. This embrace holds the promise of a revolution in narrative.When we move from the world of two dimensions to the immersive panorama of three dimensions, the spectator is presented with an opportunity to experience depth and dimension for the first time. The transition to virtual reality and augmented reality, on the other hand, brings this sensory experience to its most disorienting pinnacle. It frees the audience from the limitations of traditional screens and generously grants them the ability to engage with the story being told. Every action they do has a corresponding interactive consequence, which enables them to have a profoundly engaging and uniquely individualized experience with the narrative. They are no longer restricted to frames that have been preset, and instead become the builders of their cinematic trip.In the following discussion, I will dig into the historical progression of virtual reality and augmented reality technology as well as its essential function within the dynamic film business. To begin, I will elaborate on the delicate integration of virtual reality (VR) technology in the making of VR-centric films, therefore revealing the complexities that bring people's imaginations to life. After that, I will talk about the intriguing world of augmented reality (AR) technology and elaborate on how it has left a significant imprint in the world of filmmaking. In addition, I will walk you through an exciting film that is driven by augmented reality (AR), demonstrating how effective it is in enhancing the experience of watching a movie. After conducting an in-depth analysis of virtual reality and augmented reality in the making of films, I will conclude this section by forecasting the future of VR and AR technology within the film business and imagining the path it may take in the years to come.

The development of VR technology and VR films

Through the use of computer simulations to construct realistic, three-dimensional virtual settings, the technology known as virtual reality (VR) is revolutionizing the manner in which we perceive and interact with the digital world. Users are able to enter this virtual universe and have a sensory-rich experience that includes not only sights and sounds but also tactile sensations and other elements, therefore promoting a profound feeling of immersion. This is accomplished through the employment of external interactive equipment.

The concept of virtual reality (VR) movies is a convergence of several different types of forms of entertainment, such as movies, video games, and theaters, which has led to the development of an emerging medium. This emerging subgenre is adopting cinematic language in order to accelerate narrative breakthroughs. It does this by combining the storytelling abilities of movies with the interactive nature that is present in video games. The path that virtual reality films will take in the future appears to be heading in the direction of highly interactive and immersive dramas. In these films, the audience will have an active role in the progression of the story. User experiences are already being improved thanks to the wide variety of VR video production technologies and hardware playback devices that are already available. These advancements make it possible for users to interact more deeply within the domain of cinema. The fast development of virtual reality technology has led to the proliferation of panoramic video services that can be seen on smartphones or head-mounted displays. These services provide customers a whole fresh perspective on the material they are interested in consuming. At this time, the combination of virtual reality (VR) with cinema is still in the exploring stage. Individuals put on gadgets that are worn on their heads in order to enter the fictional world, where they are able to effortlessly immerse themselves and have the opportunity to experience a heightened sense of realism. Within this virtual reality environment, users are able to truly watch their surroundings via their own eyes and participate in certain behaviors, therefore blurring the boundaries between the virtual and the real worlds.

Virtual reality (VR) technology, when applied to the world of cinema, simulates sensory capabilities such as sight, hearing, and touch, offering a virtual experience that is both realistic and immersive. This technical marvel provides filmmakers with a tool that enables them to totally involve the audience inside the narrative, so allowing the audience members to profoundly identify with the characters and the tale. The production of virtual reality films extends beyond the capabilities of traditional recording methods, resulting in the presentation of situations that have a true sense of authenticity and the ability to evoke genuine feelings of empathy.The potential of virtual reality cinema to produce a setting that is extraordinarily immersive, one that mimics real-life experiences in a way that captivates and engrosses the audience, is a significant part of the medium's appeal. However, creators of virtual reality films have struggled with the issue of naturally incorporating audience participation into the narrative in order to achieve the goal of seamless interactivity inside their films. However, this is an area that is continually being improved upon, so current methods entail giving the audience people to identify with and integrating conversations that directly engage them.Virtual reality (VR) is essentially a new medium that is motivated by the need to have experiences that are both engaging and transformational. It has the potential to shake up the conventional methods of conveying stories in movies while also pushing the envelope of imagination and innovation. The excitement that has been generated around virtual reality is being driven by technical advancements, artificial intelligence, big data, and other developments. The inherent flexibility and subjectivity of virtual reality (VR) challenges the conventional methods of filmmaking and animation. VR presents a wholly virtual environment that is augmented by head and motion recognition technologies, delivering a level of immersion that is unsurpassed.In addition, virtual reality may be utilized outside the realm of entertainment as a powerful instrument to emotionally engage viewers with important societal concerns on a worldwide scale. The capabilities of existing near-reality 2D displays are surpassed by the capabilities of this adaptable technology, which finds ideal uses in video games, immersive movies, TV programs, and other areas. At the moment, virtual reality (VR) games and movies are at the forefront of this technological wave. Major technology firms and Hollywood are aggressively investing in the development of virtual reality (VR) experiences. The future holds the promise of an even more participatory and engaging virtual reality entertainment environment, which will be enabled by big venues, extensive motion tracking technologies, and inventive scene designs. Examples of this type of entertainment include virtual reality movies and huge virtual reality amusement parks.

Difficulties encountered in VR movie production

"The promise of virtual reality, in especially within the area of virtual reality film, is fundamentally founded in its capacity to immerse its audience. This is particularly the case. (StudioBinder, 2021) The fascinating aspect of this medium resides in the fact that it is transmissive; as a result, it effortlessly intertwines the viewer with the artwork that they engage with. Despite this, the landscape of virtual reality (VR) filmmaking is now facing a significant bottleneck. The cost is by far the most significant obstacle to overcome among the obstacles.

VR movies are broad ventures, as opposed to short, concise films; they attempt to communicate complex storylines while adding a variety of complicated special effects in their productions. At this time, the formidable challenge comes in the form of the high costs that are linked with these projects. The capabilities of traditional cameras and typical production procedures for special effects are not sufficient to allow for the creation of an all-encompassing movie with detailed special effects. Rendering effects in particular provide a big obstacle owing to the fact that they need a substantial amount of processing power, which results in longer wait times for the effects to be rendered. The current computing capability is not sufficient to fulfill these expectations, which complicates the generation of VR content by making use of devices that are already in existence.D etermining one's viewpoint is a crucial part of the art of filmmaking and represents yet another complicated aspect of the topic. Virtual reality (VR) is defined by the flexibility to modify perspective at will, giving viewers with the opportunity to explore the visual world in any manner they see appropriate. However, this independence creates a problem for the viewer, as they are not given any direction on the order in which the best moments will take place. This paradox presents a one-of-a-kind challenge: while a spectator may turn to glance what's behind them, important scenes may have already taken place elsewhere, leading to the possibility of dissatisfaction. As a consequence of this, filmmakers have a difficult time directing the attention of viewers in a way that is consistent with their aesthetic vision during the filmmaking process. The root of the problem is that moviegoers have to constantly turn their heads during the length of a two-hour movie in order to keep up with the director's plot, which may be exhausting and can cause vertigo to set in. This problem has nothing to do with a person's level of physical condition; much like motion sickness, some people have a predisposition to experience vertigo, which only adds to the difficulty of the situation.

Development and Influences of AR Technology

Augmented Reality (AR), a technical marvel at the leading edge, functions, at its core, by superimposing digital pictures onto the actual environment, so increasing the impression of reality. It creates an interactive experience by fusing together cutting-edge technology for motion tracking and feedback in a seamless manner. The primary piece of hardware required for augmented reality often takes the form of transparent glasses that have integrated image projection components. These glasses enable users to experience digital graphics superimposed on their natural environment. The powerful artificial intelligence systems that appear in the Iron Man movies serve as a remarkable example of this fusion. These systems are an illustration of the potential and integration of AR technology.

Products such as the Microsoft HoloLens are primarily accessible to developers owing to their exorbitant price point, which may reach an astounding $3000 in certain cases. As a result, the consumer market lacks a comprehensive spectrum of augmented reality (AR) technology at the present time. Despite this restriction, augmented reality glasses have demonstrated its capacity to bring game aspects into the actual environment. This has the potential to improve experiences by merging artificial opponents into the real world in a seamless manner. However, it is essential to recognize that augmented reality's ultimate potential resides outside of the realms of gaming, cinema, and television.

Instead, areas like as education and aerospace are where augmented reality is beginning to show its true promise. Augmented reality goes beyond the traditional method of displaying information about the actual world by including data from virtual worlds in a seamless manner alongside it. This symbiotic interplay between actual and virtual information increases cognition and engagement, giving a tantalizing glimpse of a science fiction future that is comparable to the magical sequences in the Harry Potter series.The broad adoption of augmented reality offers the potential to not only make our lives more comfortable, but also to make them feel more like something out of a science fiction novel. The use of augmented reality (AR) in the film business, the entertainment industry, the tourist industry, and the industry of fast-moving consumer goods (FMCG) has the potential to transform these fields. Augmented reality (AR), the newest and most promising technological breakthrough, is set to symbolize the future. AR will coexist with, but will not necessarily supersede, the established impact of television, particularly among the older age.Since the dawn of black-and-white photography until the introduction of vivid color displays, as well as from spherical screens to today's liquid crystal displays, each successive step in the evolution of picture technology has been accompanied by a discernible and noteworthy improvement in the quality of the entire viewing experience. In the present day, virtual reality (VR) adds another layer to this trend, expanding not just the size of home TVs but also the transition from a two-dimensional plane to an enticing three-dimensional environment, therefore significantly enhancing the possibilities for immersive entertainment and experiences.

The production of the AR film, NEST

Movies filmed in a virtual reality (VR) environment have grown increasingly frequent in today's media landscape, although augmented reality (AR) is not typically thought of in the same context as narrative storytelling. In spite of this, we are currently living in a period of profound change in which augmented reality (AR), virtual reality (VR), and mixed reality (MR) are advancing at a breakneck pace, ushering in novel and forward-thinking ideas. According to Gupta (2021), "the whole idea of using AR in the film is to create a world." This is an accurate statement.

Duncan Walker, the imaginative inventor of Trashgames, is responsible for the creation of an intriguing augmented reality video that piqued my interest. Filmmaking, animation, and visual effects were initially the primary focuses of Duncan's academic training early on. However, a turn in the road of events brought him into the world of programming, animation, and finally the creation of video games. Duncan is now able to combine his academic interests with the goals he has set for his professional life as a result of the recent paradigm shift brought about by virtual reality and augmented reality (VR and AR). This current moment is witnessing the progressive merging of the creative realms of cinema and video games, which is giving rise to the possibility of presenting stories in ways that have never been done before. Conventional filmmaking frequently requires actors to don motion capture suits, intricate visual effects (VFX), computerized 3D animation (CGI) characters, and elaborate post-production techniques; as a result, the production timeline is extended to several months, if not years, for rendering and the output of the final product. Nevertheless, Duncan has cleverly rethought the purpose of this custom.

At this time, people have the power to capture computer-generated characters within real-world settings and direct them in the same way that they would direct a human actor. The engaging short video that Duncan created and labeled "NEST" exemplifies this forward-thinking strategy. Aoi Nakamura, an esteemed professional dancer, consented to have a 3D scan of her face performed so that her facial traits may be recreated on a character that was developed digitally. Using ARKit on an iPhone, we were able to capture situations in real-time while integrating CGI actors and otherworldly phenomena into our reality as naturally as possible. The combination of generic situations with specific ones was where the real genius was at. During the formulaic scenes, Duncan deftly managed his CGI characters using a control interface on his phone, ordering their motions and directing their actions. On the other hand, the particular sequences were pre-designed animations, and Duncan had the ability to film them from a variety of angles and dramatic views. According to Duncan, the production of current movies is analogous to the development of video games in that there is an abundance of 3D resources, a significant amount of animation, and a decreasing dependence on actual acting. He is basically a game engineer, since he is responsible for the creation of game characters and the subsequent transformation of these characters into cinematic experiences. At the moment, these CGI figures tend to imitate simulated character movements, and they lack emotional depth. Despite this, Duncan maintains a positive outlook because of the rapid progress being made in the field of AI machine learning. He believes that the incorporation of feelings into computer-generated characters is not too far off in the near future. Soon, these avatars will have the capacity to engage convincingly with real-life actors, much in the same way that self-driving cars are able to accurately observe and respond to the surroundings in which they find themselves. Duncan draws attention to the fact that the character's capabilities are analogous to those of a smartphone. He wants to improve the software's image analysis skills on the iPhone so that it can support real-time picture processing. This will ultimately lead to an improvement in the quality of the finished result. At this time, the finished work is sent to traditional 2D platforms such as YouTube, movie theaters, or television. Notable is the fact that "NEST" had its debut at the prestigious Raindance Film Festival in 2017, having been filmed using an iPhone 7 with ARKit and Unity. Even while "NEST" will continue to be a 2D film, Duncan imagines a future in which people will be able to download an app onto their cellphones that would allow them to see the movie unfold in their actual environments. Duncan's goals include continuing his exploration into augmented reality (AR) filmmaking, with the overarching objective of developing a toolbox with the intention of enabling other filmmakers to create their own fascinating AR movies and therefore transforming the field of storytelling.

The role of VR/AR in the film industry and the development trend

Virtual Reality (VR) and Augmented Reality (AR) cinema represent a paradigm shift in the realms of technology and artistic expression. This shift is comparable to significant historical shifts such as the introduction of sound to film, the transition from black-and-white to color, or the shift from two-dimensional imagery to three-dimensional experiences. According to what Schutze stated in 2018, these new "realities" are not only the result of developments in technology; rather, they herald the beginning of a new age in terms of communication and entertainment.

The transition from painting to sculpture or photography to film may be seen as parallels to the one that virtual reality and augmented reality have brought about in the film industry, which is an intriguing parallel to consider. It allows the cinematic experience to be manifested into a three-dimensional environment, which is a break from the traditional limits of a two-dimensional screen. It encompasses a departure from these usual confines. Virtual reality and augmented reality cinema is a development that, at its core, extends an invitation to viewers to immerse themselves in storylines that come to life in a way that is very physical and participatory. However, despite the enormous potential and promise it has, virtual reality and augmented reality cinema is still in a precarious stage of development. VR/AR cinema, on the other hand, is still in its infant phases and is struggling to define a mature model for storytelling and cinematography. This is in contrast to traditional filmmaking, which has narrative and camera language paradigms that have been established. Notably, the VR/AR filmmaking technology that is now available is incapable of reaching the stringent requirements that are imposed by traditional film production. This presents a significant barrier to the broad acceptance and popularization of VR/AR movies in the near future. The road ahead for virtual reality and augmented reality movies will require not only the development of new technologies, but also the progression of aesthetic and narrative conventions concurrently. The potential for immersive narrative in a three-dimensional setting is becoming increasingly accessible as the capabilities of VR/AR devices continue to advance and filmmakers develop a greater grasp of how to harness these technologies. The convergence of innovative technology and creative expression holds the key to realizing the full potential of virtual reality and augmented reality movies and bringing it to the attention of the general public. This will forever alter the landscape of entertainment and communication for future generations.

What We Need to Know About Globalization of the Film Industry

The sphere of the film business undoubtedly reveals itself to be comprised of several levels, some of which are beyond our immediate awareness; one of the most notable of these layers is undoubtedly globalization. The concept of globalization, which goes much beyond that of simple internationalization, describes a significant process. It involves more than the diffusion of products, personalities, or techniques from a single or a handful of nations; rather, it exemplifies a sophisticated web of relationships tying together a number of different nations. These links, in turn, lead to their amalgamation into a single or possibly numerous global economic, cultural, and to some extent political frameworks or networks (as elucidated upon by academics such as Held et al., 1999; Friedman, 2000; Stiglitz, 2002; Amin and Cohendet, 2004). A recent investigation that is both thought-provoking and accessible may be found in a volume and issue of Industry and Innovation devoted entirely to the topic of knowledge geographies (Volume 12, Issue 4, 2004).Let's go into a revealing investigation of a few aspects relating to the globalization of the film business so that we may better understand it. These include a detailed investigation into the effects of globalization in the areas of 1) active engagement in the filmmaking process; 2) the patterns of film consumption; 3) the dynamics of film production; and 4) the organizational structure of the filmmaking sphere. Among these are some of the most important aspects of the filmmaking industry. By studying these important components, we want to gain a better understanding of the far-reaching implications that globalization has had on the complex web that is the film business.

Globalization of involvement in film-making

The first element may be clearly explained, and that is the significant transition that is currently taking place in filmmaking toward public engagement all across the world. Outside of the confines of the United States, there has been a boom in the creation of feature films that will be shown in theaters, on television, and on a variety of other exhibition platforms. This expansion is not limited to the substantial nations that have historically been heavily involved in film production, such as China and India, where the annual release numbers have shown a consistent increase for over a decade now. Instead, it includes all nations that are now experiencing growth. According to information provided by Lorenzen and Taeube in 2008, the driving force behind this uptick may be traced to the rising spending power of consumers as well as the large expenditures made in theaters and other exhibition venues.

A major increase in film output has been seen in a number of less populated countries that, in the past, have depended on state subsidies for their film industries. This is in addition to the growth of the film industry in these more populous countries. This may be seen when seen through the perspective of policy shifts and newly discovered financing opportunities, both of which were comprehensively explored in 2007 by Kaiser and Liecke and Morawetz et al., respectively. Notably, European countries such as Denmark, Switzerland, and Iceland have received attention not just for increasing their production capabilities but also for effectively snatching a section of their domestic markets from the preeminent Hollywood sector. This accomplishment has allowed these nations to attract a great deal of attention in recent years. In addition, the landscape of cinema is experiencing a shift in some countries that are only beginning to develop their film industries.Film production is witnessing a considerable uptick in these countries, which range from the flourishing art film scenes in Korea and Mexico to the expanding video industries in Brazil and Nigeria. This upswing is made possible by the emergence of new exhibition locations and the accessibility of production technologies that are more efficient with regards to cost. The convergence of these variables is altering the global film business and bringing about an era of worldwide cinematic involvement on a scale that has never been seen before.

Globalization of consumption

The second aspect of globalization is the rapidly growing diversity of tastes held by consumers throughout the world, as well as the proliferation of consumer goods. Not only are mainstream markets expanding consistently on a worldwide basis, but film makers now also have the ability to engage with specialized audiences at the same time, which is an important development. These specialized audience groups include fans of art, Kung Fu, Manga, and other ethnic Diasporas living in a variety of nations throughout the world. As a consequence of this, the landscape of cinema export is experiencing a shift. This transition is taking place from the typical progressive internationalization of films that are made for home audiences and are then distributed in other markets, to an encompassing phenomena that occurs all over the world. Films that are intended for viewers all around the world are now released simultaneously in a number of different national markets. Even while Hollywood has made significant efforts to be at the forefront of this evolutionary process, film makers from other parts of the world are becoming increasingly involved. As a consequence of this, the patterns of film export are morphing into increasingly complex configurations; despite this, the question of whether or not the general spike in exports from nations like India and China can be maintained indefinitely remains unanswered. In a similar vein, the sporadic export successes of countries like Korea and Spain raise questions about the long-term prospects of those countries.New distribution and exhibition channels, such as satellite television, DVD releases, and the Internet, all of which have the power to engage specialized audiences on a worldwide scale, have been a major factor in the globalization of consumption. This process has been significantly aided by these mediums. For instance, cinema genres such as art, Kung Fu, and Manga today attract devoted cult followings all around the world, while not fitting neatly into any conventional demographic category. In the case of Indian films, their audience has broadened to include members of the growing Indian diaspora in countries such as the United Kingdom, the United States of America, and Canada. This is an indication of the widespread influence that globalization has had on the patterns of consumer behavior. According to Currah (2007), countries that have prominent film industries, such as Japan and India, have demonstrated a proactive attitude in leveraging new technologies for distribution and exhibition, surpassing Hollywood in this respect. Japan and India are only two examples of such countries. As a consequence of this, the globalization of consumption is eventually accelerated by cinema firms across a spectrum of nations, who are gradually devoting considerable capital towards production, marketing, and distribution. These coordinated initiatives reflect incremental steps toward bridging the gap with Hollywood's early investments and economies of scale, and they are progressing in the right direction.

Globalization of production

The third aspect of globalization relates to the interweaving of cinema projects across international boundaries. This aspect of globalization is captured by the phrase "Global productions." There has been a recent uptick in the number of cross-border co-productions, despite the fact that these kinds of projects have been around for a century. A paradigm change may be seen in the film business as a result of the frequent international cooperation among Asian, Canadian, and European film companies. An enlightening example of this tendency may be found in the in-depth investigation of co-productions within the German filmmaking sector that is presented in Kaiser and Liecke's (2007) study. This study was published in 2007.

According to the findings of Norbert Morawetz and colleagues (2007), worldwide co-productions frequently take place for a wide variety of reasons. Some are inspired just by imagination, with the intention of incorporating particular locations or making use of specialized knowledge. They simultaneously make it possible for production companies from several countries to combine their financial resources and creative resources in a single pool. On the other hand, a sizeable chunk is conceived with the intention of making the most of the attractive tax advantages and national cinema promotion policies that are available.Concerns have been raised by observers, particularly those working in the Hollywood industry, about the trajectory of international collaboration as it now stands (Wright, 2006). However, Hollywood companies demonstrate a remarkable adeptness, similar to that of its Indian counterparts, in combing the world for prospects for regional or national film funding that give financial incentives. This is something that their Indian competitors also do. This strategy makes it easier to entice filming initiatives and other activities linked with filmmaking from other countries. The outsourcing of "runaway" production tasks to alternative film clusters that show cost-effectiveness is another aspect of production globalization that is led by Hollywood (Coe, 2001; Wasko, 2003; Coe and Johns 2004; Scott, 2005; Flew, 2007). This aspect of production globalization was pioneered by Hollywood (Coe, 2001; Wasko, 2003; Coe and Johns 2004; Scott, 2005; Flew, 2007).There may be qualitatively different effects brought about by this new paradigm for global cinema production on film clusters all over the world that are afterwards incorporated into the framework of globalization. Some clusters continue to keep their one-of-a-kind film production skills or offer unmatched levels of knowledge as opposed to just offering cost benefits; this is a point that is made abundantly obvious by the results of Vang and Chaminade (2007). This evolution not only reshapes the structure of film production but also challenges conventional dynamics, opening the way for a dynamic and interconnected cinema environment on a worldwide scale. This evolution not only reshapes the structure of film production but also challenges traditional dynamics.

Global organization

The creation of new forms of organization on a global scale is the subject of the fourth and last aspect of globalization that will be investigated in depth. The emergence of multinational businesses stands out as one of these trends' most visible manifestations. These multinational behemoths have significantly expanded their reach and spheres of influence, therefore changing the competitive environment in a variety of business sectors.

As was said before, production businesses situated in Hollywood were the ones that blazed the way by extending their activities across international borders, achieving seamless integration across a variety of industries, and developing into multifunctional multimedia organizations. Notably, a considerable number of these organizations have been a part of acquisitions or mergers, frequently forming connections with corporate behemoths headquartered in nations such as France, Japan, and Australia. The resultant multinational corporations, which originated mostly in Hollywood but also included a number of second-tier equivalents from Europe or Japan, have acquired worldwide ownership and a broad operational scope as a result. These firms are responsible for the majority of the industry's profits.Their hegemony encompasses a wide range of national markets, and it extends to the financing, marketing, and distribution of films and other types of connected media. However, it is essential to recognize that the rise of large multinational firms has not occurred in the same manner in every region of the world. They have established a preeminent presence in a wide range of nations, and its distribution and marketing subsidiaries are highly effective, allowing them to provide a diverse selection of global products, most of which originate in the United States, to the markets in those countries. On the other hand, only a small number of countries see the presence of big multinational firms since there are local production companies there whose sole mission is to create native content on a relatively modest budget that is intended solely for consumption on the local level.In addition, multinational firms are engaged in the practice of aggressively scouting a limited number of nations in search of emerging talent and goods that have the potential to be sold on a worldwide scale. With the end goal of worldwide distribution in mind, many strategies are utilized, including co-creation of high-budget films in partnership with regional production businesses. In addition to the more obvious expression of multinational firms and ownership structures, globalization also gives rise to a type of global organization that is more covert but nevertheless substantial.This hidden form has its origins in the constantly shifting landscape of product innovation that exists inside the film business. Given the ephemeral and fluid nature of innovative initiatives within this sector, the industry places a significant amount of emphasis on complex and loosely organized social networks. These networks are made up of people who have worked together on prior projects. As a result, they are built on a foundation of mutual trust, which frequently paves the way for more partnerships in the future.These social networks have also increased their reach beyond international borders, which coincides with an increase in the number of projects in the film industry that take place on a worldwide scale, as well as an increase in the movement of talent across a variety of nations and film clusters. The globalization of the sector is matched by the globalization of these complex social ties, highlighting the interconnectivity of persons and businesses in a world that is becoming more international.

Future research on Globalization of the Film Industry

Our comprehension of the globalization of the film business that is currently taking place is, to some extent, still relatively restricted. Our perspective has been clouded because we have been concentrating on a small number of important characteristics, such as minimum market sizes, demand uncertainty, and scale economies, all of which impact specialization and internationalization. Because of the United States film industry's preeminent success, there are not nearly enough studies that are all-encompassing and that go beyond the confines of Hollywood. At a high level, there is an urgent need to conceptualize and carry out quantitative studies to discover if the previously established conceptions related minimum profitable market sizes, demand uncertainty, and scale economies are experiencing adjustments in the period of globalization. This is because there is a pressing need to ascertain whether the previously established notions are undergoing shifts.

For example, the development of novel distribution and exhibition technologies, such as pay-per-view television and Internet streaming, has the potential to enable film distributors to tap into and derive profits from niche audiences that constitute the "long tail" in the scale-free distrib- ution of demand for a variety of film products (Hesmondhalgh, 2002; Anderson, 2006). This is made possible by the advent of technologies such as DVDs, pay-per-view television, and Internet streaming. In ad- dition, because globalization is taking the shape of newly formed global networks, there is an urgent need to get a deeper understanding of these networks as they emerge. Linkages are one of the most important aspects of these networks that calls for close examination.links in global networks are described through diverse organizational forms on a worldwide scale. These organizational forms range from formal network links, which are represented by global companies, to informal network linkages, which are expressed by social relations. The study of social interactions lends itself to a variety of analytical techniques; nevertheless, case studies are particularly useful for gaining insights into the histories, paths, and obstacles encoun- tered by organizations in the course of their worldwide operations. This entails doing research on the local links that exist among the many stake- holders of the film industry within a particular cluster or nation, as well as assessing how the structure of networks that are generated by these link- ages effects product innovation and project performance. This component has risen to prominence among cinema economists and sociologists, who utilize databases on film projects and participants for the purpose of con- ducting extensive research (for example, Baker and Faulkner, 1991; Soda et al., 2004; Delmestri et al., 2005; Sorenson and Waguespack, 2006).

However, there are considerable data issues involved in studying non-lo- cal links across different clusters and nations, as well as understanding how these linkages stretch when individuals travel between clusters and countries. In addition to statistical methodologies, case studies that depict worldwide careers that span many film clusters (Morgan, 2001; Saxenian, 2002) may be able to give insightful complementary information. The nodes that are a part of this network are an additional vital component of the ever-expanding worldwide networks that are present in the film indus try.In spite of the undeniable fact that the film industry is in the process of transforming into a worldwide network, academics have divergent points of view about the relevance of the nodes in this network, which are film clusters. (Bakker, 2005; Epstein, 2006; Currah, 2007) There is a school of thought that maintains that the significance of clusters is waning as a direct result of the proliferation of broad worldwide networks. Others, on the other hand, argue that both global corporations and clusters continue to play equally pivotal roles in the cultural industries, asserting a new global division of labor (Scott, 2000; 2005; Flew, 2007; Cooke and Lazzeretti, 2007). This viewpoint is supported by broader claims about labor markets that were made by Florida (2005). Comprehensive case studies that focus on demand shifts, alterations in export and performance, organization-al transformations, and policies within robust film clusters and coun-tries—such as India, China, Taiwan, and Korea—become imperative in order to enhance our understanding and facilitate the development of theory concerning the roles of nodes in the burgeoning global networks within the film industry. This will allow us to better understand and facilitate the development of theories concerning the roles of nodes in these networks.One empirical technique that appears to be particularly suited for increasing our knowledge is to go outside Hollywood. This is despite the fact that the aim of investigating the varied facets of the ongoing globalization of the film industry is an enormous one. In essence, this entails conducting research on and making comparisons between various national cinema industries. These sectors range from commercial to state-subsidized, small-scale to large-scale, integrated to fragmented. For instance, Hollywood and Bollywood are both examples of commercial and large-scale operations, but with varying degrees of integration. Both of these places are located in California. In a similar vein, both Denmark and Korea are examples of small-scale and fragmented sectors, but with varied degrees of engagement from the state. On the other hand, Iceland and France are examples of models that combine official support with private enterprise, albeit on a smaller scale in France.It is imperative to give due consideration to this burgeoning global diversity within the film industry in order to begin the process of unraveling global linkages between individuals and locations and to comprehend the emergence of new global practices and networks that may ultimately reshape the known patterns of specialization and organization within the film industry. In addition, in order to begin the process of unraveling global linkages between individuals and locations, it is necessary to begin the process of unraveling global linkages between individuals and locations. We may pave the way for a deeper knowledge of the changing global dynamics and the profound consequences they have for the future of the film industry on a global scale by conducting an exhaustive examination of the various variables involved.

What are TV Distribution models?

Find out how the different models work and what's in store for satellite

The landscape of television distribution has seen substantial adjustments over the course of many decades, signifying a break from old patterns. These changes have been brought about by advances in technology. The modern period provides us with a wide variety of channels via which we may have access to various forms of entertainment as well as information. These channels are all classified as falling under the umbrella term of "television," which we typically refer to as a more general term. In spite of this, it is interesting to note that the once-dominant Satellite TV platform has not only been able to survive, but is really thriving despite all of the changes that have taken place.

The paradigm of television distribution has evolved to incorporate a variety of cutting-edge delivery mechanisms in recent times, expanding beyond the scope of traditional terrestrial broadcasts to include a wider range of options. The proliferation of streaming services, on-demand platforms, and internet-based applications has made it possible for viewers to personalize their viewing experiences according to their tastes and the schedules they have available. Because of this change in consumption habits, some people are wondering whether or not traditional television services that are dependent on satellite will remain relevant in the future.

In contrast to these preconceived beliefs, satellite television has shown to be remarkably resilient and adaptable in the face of the rapidly shifting dynamics of the terrain in which TV distribution occurs. There are a number of reasons that contribute to its ongoing popularity. To begin, satellite broadcasting's expansive coverage assures a wide reach, particularly in secluded or geographically tough locations where terrestrial signals may be weak or nonexistent. This is because satellites can reach places terrestrial signals cannot. This advantage is essential for bridging the digital divide and guaranteeing that viewers in a variety of places can watch television material without any interruptions or difficulties. In addition, satellite television continues to be a trustworthy option for live broadcasts of important events, such as sporting events, news, and specialized programming. Because of their speed and consistency, satellite broadcasts are quickly becoming the medium of choice for broadcasting live material to large groups of people at the same time. In an era where "live" is more prized, satellite technology stands as a stalwart, guaranteeing that viewers don't miss out on significant events that are taking place all over the world.In addition, developments in satellite technology have helped strengthen its advantage over other technologies. Transmissions in high-definition (HD) and ultra-high-definition (UHD) have become the norm, which offers viewers a greater visual experience. In addition to this, providers of satellite television have begun including interactive elements, making it possible to have a viewing experience that is both more interesting and more uniquely your own. Viewers may now vote in polls, have access to more information about their favorite programs, and even engage in conversation with other fans in real time.In addition, in order to accommodate the shifting preferences of customers, satellite television service providers have included internet streaming capabilities into their various packages. The best of both worlds may be offered to viewers by utilizing hybrid models that combine internet-based content distribution with satellite broadcasts. This provides viewers with access to a complete and varied selection of programming. This modification to accommodate shifting tendencies exemplifies the industry's forward-thinking strategy and dedication to satisfying the requirements of an audience that is knowledgeable about tec hnology.To summarize, the transformation of TV distribution methods into a landscape with several facets has not marked the end of the line for satellite television. Instead, it has prompted creative problem-solving inside the satellite business, which has strengthened the sector's importance and ensured its continued expansion. Consumers who are interested in having an all-encompassing television experience should continue to consider satellite television as a viable alternative because it is dependable, extensive, and technologically advanced. As the world of television continues to advance, there is little question that satellite television will advance with it, continuing to be an essential component of our enjoyment and the distribution of information.

How we receive TV

Many of us enjoy the benefits of television-based entertainment and information but have no idea of how or why it works. TV distribution itself can come in many different shapes and sizes, but there are three main types of delivery models:

- Satellite Direct-to-Home

- Terrestrial networks (e.g. Cable, IP and DTT distribution)

- OTT (Over-the-Top)

Let's take a closer look at each one in more detail.

Satellite Direct-to-Home (DTH)

Direct-to-Home (DTH) transmission via satellite is widely regarded as one of the simplest and most effective methods for disseminating television programs using satellite technology. This method of distribution includes the sending of video content through radio waves, which are then picked up by a satellite dish that is normally mounted on the roof of the home where the content is being viewed.

The direct distribution of channels to the television set of the viewer is one of the most significant benefits offered by direct-to-home (DTH) systems. Because of this, a separate cable connection is no longer required in order to have access to a diverse range of television channels. Additionally, the use of this kind of broadcasting breaks down the constraints that are imposed by geography, allowing broadcasters to reach substantially more people. DTH guarantees that broadcasters may effectively reach and serve viewers, even in the most distant corners of a country, therefore providing a service that is really available across the nation, regardless of the amount of infrastructural development in that country.

When seen from the point of view of the broadcaster, satellite television has a unique advantage in terms of both its reach and its efficiency in terms of cost. Satellite broadcasting is unique among transmission infrastructures in that its costs remain the same regardless of the size of the viewer base. This is in contrast to the majority of other transmission infrastructures. Although the initial expenditure may be seen as a disadvantage, the instant access to a very large number of houses makes it a point-to-multipoint network option that is exceptionally effective for broadcasters.T he level of technological development of DTH is an important area of concern for broadcasters. Nevertheless, direct-to-home (DTH) watching is witnessing tremendous expansion across a variety of countries despite these issues. Notably, direct-to-home (DTH) technology may accommodate a wide variety of codecs, including the 4k format, which offers a very high resolution. Broadcasters are given the capacity to transmit a large number of channels in high quality because to the vast bandwidth that is made available through satellite transmission. This is a feat that is not readily accomplished through alternative distribution techniques, since these options frequently impose limits on the number of channels that can be maintained.The benefits of direct-to-home television are numerous and extensive. The transmission of the signal in its purest form, unaltered by any cable splits, assures that the material will be of the highest possible quality. In addition, viewers have the flexibility to choose without the influence of a middleman, as there is no cable operator to restrict the channel possibilities that are available to them. The only recurrent expense normally associated with DTH is the initial hardware expenditure, which makes it an appealing offer for viewers who are interested in free-to-air TV channels because it can prove to be cost-effective for them.However, it is essential to keep in mind that the viewing experience of viewers differs from one location to another and from one business model to another. In certain locations, it is possible to obtain access to a large number of free television channels with a low initial investment, while in other regions, the installation of the receiving gear may be more expensive and require more time and effort to complete. This disparity highlights the impact that regional characteristics and corporate tactics have on the Direct-to-Home (DTH) experience that viewers have.

Terrestrial networks

Terrestrial networks play a pivotal role in the dissemination of television signals, acting as a conduit for channel reception at the network head-end, subsequently redistributing these channels to subscribing viewers. This transmission is often facilitated through satellite-based mechanisms, a process commonly referred to as headend feeding.

These terrestrial networks encompass three primary variants:

1. Cable Networks:

A term denoting the delivery of video content via coaxial cable con-nections. This established technology has been a foundational method for transmitting television signals to households, utilizing a network of cables to deliver a multitude of channels.

2. IP Networks:

IP networks utilize the internet to deliver video content through privately managed networks. This method capitalizes on the extensive reach and accessibility of the internet, enabling efficient delivery of video streams to viewers.

3. Digital Terrestrial Networks:

These networks rely on radio waves to deliver video content, which is received through a digital set-top box, a TV gateway, or an integrated tuner included with a television set. This method employs modern technology to ensure a clear and high-quality signal for viewers.

For broadcasters, the main challenges lie in the limitations related to reach and content availability. Terrestrial networks heavily depend on the existing infrastructure within a country. Consequently, remote areas are often beyond the reach of these networks due to inadequate or costly-to-deploy terrestrial infrastructure. To mitigate this, broadcasters often utilize satellites to extend their service coverage, thereby maximizing their reach to a broader audience.Moreover, both cable and IP networks face constraints in terms of the number of channels they can support. This limitation is significantly lower compared to satellite-based options, which offer a more extensive channel capacity, providing a broader array of content choices to viewers.In areas where cable, IP, or terrestrial networks are accessible, viewers enjoy easy access to a reliable stream of content. However, this convenience is not universal, particularly in regions where coverage is lacking. The availability of bandwidth and diverse content offerings is contingent on the viewer's location, resulting in varied experiences for individuals based on their geographical context and network accessibility.

Over-the-Top (OTT)

"Over-The-Top," abbreviated as "OTT," is an industry term that refers to the process of transmitting video information across the vast expanse of the public internet. OTT is a relatively new paradigm. As an alternative to the more conventional cable and satellite providers, over-the-top (OTT) services make use of the rapid and effective conduit provided by high-speed internet connections. It is essential, however, to dispel the impression that over-the-top (OTT) stands for free access because within its scope lie significant platforms such as Netflix, Amazon, iTunes, and HBO Now, all of which operate according to subscription-based business models.

Although consumers may effortlessly access OTT material through a variety of mediums, including PCs, the majority of its consumption is witnessed through web-enabled televisions or internet-connected devices such as Roku or Apple TV, which interface neatly with traditional television settings.Two of the most important advantages that over-the-top (OTT) services provide are low prices and the flexibility to watch shows and movies whenever you want to. Its attraction may be summed up in two words: cost-effectiveness for viewers, along with the freedom to customize their viewing experience in accordance with their own tastes. However, broadcasters are faced with a subtle task as they navigate the multifaceted terrain that this digital revolution has created.

The pay-per-user model that is inherent to OTT platforms runs into a phenomena known as a tipping point, particularly when the platform achieves tremendous success and amasses a growing following. The ever-increasing expenses of using a Content Delivery Network (CDN), which are proportional to the growing number of viewers, are the primary source of the problem. This is in sharp contrast to the dynamics of satellite services, which see relatively stable operational expenses despite an increase in the number of viewers. Satellite services have a clear advantage in this regard. As a direct result of this, over-the-top (OTT) distribution eventually climbs the expenditure ladder to a point where it is no longer affordable to use satellite services.In addition, the benefits of OTT are cancelled out by the inherent unpredictability of the situation. When travelling through a landscape that is aggressively disputed by several content producers, there is no assurance that users will be able to see certain material. Limitations in bandwidth create a detectable shadow on the overall quality of the information, while latency concerns offer perceptible time delays in live event broadcasts. In addition, end-users have to contend with the necessity of a stable internet connection in order to guarantee uninterrupted reception of the broadcast, which is a luxury that is not generally available.Broadcasters face a complex obstacle that is made more difficult by the stringent requirements of internet availability as they work toward their goal of maximizing the benefits of over-the-top (OTT) delivery. A resilient network backbone that is able to provide stability across a range of circumstances is necessary in order to lay the groundwork for a solid and dependable over-the-top (OTT) viewing experience. Even in a country as technologically advanced as France, a sizeable section of the population struggles with slow connection speeds, which prevents them from fully capitalizing on the possibilities of over-the-top (OTT) content from the convenience of their own homes.The over-the-top (OTT) service providers are expanding their strategies in response to this problem. For example, they are investigating alternate routes, such as satellite technology, to broaden their customer base and improve the dependability of their streaming services. They hope that by doing so, they will be able to eliminate the digital gap and ensure that a larger proportion of the world's population will be able to take part in the rapidly expanding digital entertainment scene.

The future of TV distribution

With the extensive media coverage of services such as Netflix, it would be expected that OTT would be undisputed as the future of TV distribution models. However, this is simply not the case. Satellite TV distribution is in fact rapidly growing, both in emerging markets such as Africa, South America and parts of Europe and in more mature markets such as the USA, UK and Australia.

Here are a few points to consider on the facts of satellite service today.

Satellite audience continues to grow

The satellite market has continued to maintain its share of over a quarter of the total market and is expected to increase its share by around 4% over the next three years .

Broadcasters continue to choose satellite distribution for its extensive reach and scaling capabilities. Unlike other forms of distribution, satellites can offer a multitude of channels and reach more audience members in a more cost-effective way than OTT. This fact was highlighted in our MENA webinar by Michael Cairns, COO of Rotana Media when he said, "As a broadcasting technology to reach a mass market in an economical way, satellite provides that possibility and will continue to do so.

The build out of other networks to address 100% of the population won't happen fast enough."

Satellite is the preferred choice for Africa

Including 7 of the 10 world's fastest growing economies, African homes are predominantly choosing satellite above other forms of distribution methods. This is due to the more remote nature of many households in Africa as well as the minimal infrastructure required to support quality local and international TV viewing. Satellite offer these channels visibility, stability and quality which other forms of distribution are unable to support.

OTT broadcasters are turning to satellite to extend their reach

OTT broadcasters are increasingly seeing satellite television as an opportunity rather than a threat. Satellite offers OTT broadcasters a new way to reach thousands of homes and expand their audience. In Germany, sports streaming service DAZN is looking to distribute its linear channels to Sky subscribers to reach more homes. According to Ampere Analysis Insights, this would enable DAZN to access an additional 1.9 million households and potentially generate up to €153 million in revenue. And in France, Netflix recently announced that they are testing their first linear channel to meet consumer demand for "traditional TV" in the country. In essence, OTT operators are starting to consider the benefits of hybrid networks to gain more reach and access all viewers across countries.

Satellite will continue to be the fastest way to access a stable subscriber base

Digital TV Research analysis shows that in mature markets Pay-TV satellite subscriber numbers will continue to remain stable for the next five years, while free-to-air satellite subscribers are growing year on year.

5G is unready - but will always rely on satellite

5G continues to remain expensive for broadcasters, and currently does not offer the coverage broadcasters are looking for. Despite this, satellites will always be needed to feed the 5G head-ends, and many consumers will simply not be able to afford 5G in its current form.

Satellite coverage and access continues to grow

Finally, the total number of TV homes is expected to increase by over 70 million to 1.76 billion by 2023. When it comes to satellite reception, 20 million more homes will have access to satellite, bringing the total number to an impressive 450 million by 2023.No matter how popular OTT becomes, satellite continues to grow in contrast to other distribution models such as cable. Broadcasters who wish to capitalise on emerging markets around the world could seize an opportunity to access viewers through satellite.

Partner with the best - reach the rest

Satellite distribution is a unique and beneficial channel for broadcasters. It provides an unrivaled chance for broadcasters to seamlessly interact with TV markets in a manner that transcends the efficiency and directness of other distribution methods. Satellite distribution is a distinct and advantageous route for broadcasters. The capabilities of satellite technology extend to the furthest reaches of houses, even travelling into the most inaccessible areas, allowing users to gain access to a wide variety of television channels and other types of entertainment.In view of this strong potential, broadcasters are coming to the realization that it is important for them to adopt a hybrid method, which combines satellite distribution with terrestrial distribution. This strategic merger offers as a dynamic solution to handle the changing environment of demand for bandwidth and coverage that is on the future. By integrating these components in such a way that they complement one another, broadcasters are able to efficiently overcome hurdles, which in turn ensures that their content repertoire is maximized, that their audience receives more exposure, and that they have a better overall user experience.Mentioning Eutelsat is essential for everyone who is interested in capitalizing on this constantly increasing sector. As new markets sprout up all over the world, Eutelsat establishes itself as the leading provider of satellite services. This propels the company to the forefront of the industry. Eutelsat permits broadcasters to expand their reach to a multitude of households by virtue of the well-structured constellation of terrestrial and extra-terrestrial satellites that it has at its disposal. This magnifies the efficacy of engagement and penetration into the market. By taking use of the services provided by Eutelsat, broadcasters will be able to successfully traverse the ever-changing environment of the broadcasting industry and will be able to establish a strong footing in the bright future of satellite distribution.

CHAPTER THREE

Film Industry's Influence on Society

The positive effects of movies on human behaviour

Films are a sort of visual storytelling that occupy a large position in the lives of many people. Like music or other hobbies, watching films and participating in conversations about them can provide a lot of enjoyment to those who watch them. The world of filmmaking is home to a plethora of tales, each of which has the potential to have a diverse range of effects on a person's life, including enhancing, diminishing, or even just having no noticeable effect at all. In our contemporary period, which is distinguished by the presence of Over-The-Top (OTT) Platforms, a number of film subgenres have garnered enormous popularity, enthralling people all over the world. These categories include Anime, Drama, Comedy, Horror, Fantasy, and Action, and each of these subgenres has a distinct appeal of its own.

There is much food for thought to be had on the impact that these film subgenres, in particular, have had on the younger audience. Young people's imaginations are frequently captivated by anime due to the genre's unique animation style and wide range of narratives; this helps foster creative thinking and increases cultural sensitivity. Drama, by virtue of its representation of human feelings and experiences, acts as a mirror to society, so encouraging empathy and a greater knowledge of the ways in which people behave. On the other side, comedy is an excellent way to release some of the tension and anxiety that comes with daily living, since it encourages laughing and happiness.

The domain of Horror, however, can be found within this vast assortment of genres, and it is the realm that inspires both terror and excitement, sometimes resulting in restless nights and heightened tension. humans may be transported to fresh and exciting realms by fantasy, with its inventive and frequently magical features. While this can fuel creativity in humans, it also has the ability to alienate them from reality. Action movies, with their heart-pounding set pieces and characters that are larger than life, imbue viewers with a sense of heroism and the desire to go on daring adventures.Studies and research have been conducted in an effort to determine the overall influence that these types of media have on persons, particularly the young and those who are impressionable. According to the findings of certain research, watching movies that include a lot of violence might make people more aggressive and could even prompt them to engage in risky conduct. This perspective highlights the necessity of exercising caution and restraint in movie watching, particularly for individuals who are prone to being unduly influenced by what they watch. On the other hand, other research attempts highlight the educational potential of certain films and advocate for their usage in academic contexts to boost students' learning and critical thinking abilities. The scales are finely balanced in the discussion about the benefits and drawbacks of going to the movies. There is not one single opinion that unequivocally supports either the positive or negative outcomes that result from watching movies. It is a multifaceted landscape in which one's own preferences, cultural influences, and unique psychological make-up all come together to create one's opinion on the topic. Because of this, the influence of movies continues to be a fluid and multi-dimensional phenomena, which exemplifies the requirement for discernment and a mindful approach to the consumption of movies in the modern culture.

Some instances of how movies can be beneficial to watch:

1] Violence Reduction:

Unquestionably, in the current state of the film industry, the subgenre of drama is the one that has the most influence on spectators and is most successful at inspiring their imaginations. This widespread preference is especially obvious among the younger generation, which has a significant interest in stories that are filled with whispers, intrigues, portrayals of violence, investigations of complicated relationships, and confrontations with situations of bullying, among other topics.

A multiplicity of individuals emerge as fascinating role models inside the fabric of current dramas, and these personalities leave an unforgettable effect on the brains of sensitive youth. The impact of these characters goes beyond the constraints of the silver screen, as the youth frequently find themselves copying the acts and behaviors of their on-screen idols. This shows that the influence of these characters extends beyond the confines of the silver screen. This phenomena exemplifies the significant influence that movies may have on the formative years of an individual, influencing not only their views but also their behavior in relation to other people and the larger society.

This particular subgenre of filmmaking is notable for its ability to shed light on the sharp difference between good and evil, which is one of its most notable advantages. When young brains are immersed in the storylines that are woven by these films, they are presented with a spectrum of moral dimensions, which enables them to recognize the ethical foundations that drive human acts. This discernment, in turn, helps in the growth of an educated ethical compass, which assists young people in navigating the complex maze that is life with a fuller knowledge of the repercussions that may be entailed by the choices that they make.In addition to developing moral insights, plays frequently act as catalysts for critical thinking and the development of autonomous thought. This benefit extends beyond the simple act of fostering moral insights. These films, with their complicated storylines and multifaceted characters, provoke thought and inspire the audience to participate in self-reflection by posing questions that demand thoughtful consideration. By wrestling with the conundrums that are depicted on the screen, the audience is encouraged to hone their ability to make decisions, which instills in them the fortitude that is necessary to make choices in their own lives that are sensible and well-considered.In conclusion, the modern public's enduring love affair with drama as the premier cinematic genre is evidence of the genre's uncanny capacity to speak to the ever-evolving preferences and sensitivities of the audience, particularly the younger generation. Drama provides a fundamental platform for moral enlightenment, molding young minds and enabling them to discriminate between good and evil, while also promoting the development of critical thinking abilities that are important for navigating the complexity of current living. Drama's benefits extend well beyond those of a simple kind of entertainment.

2] Educational Importance

Students who skip school on purpose or drop out of school altogether might get a glimpse of the future they are creating for themselves via the lens of modern instructional films. These depictions in film frequently feature individuals that are struggling with a mediocre educational background, which leads to a life that is distinguished by discontent or restricted career options. There is a common thread that runs through all of these films, and it relates to the idea that those who forgo their education are more likely to struggle in life and have less chances available to them.The degree to which today's kids are responsive to the lessons that are being sent to them through films like these is a noteworthy trend. Surprisingly, the impact of advice from parents, extended family, or even close friends is typically less effective than the power of narratives on television and in movies. In this day and age of ubiquitous media consumption, the medium of visual storytelling possesses considerable power and is capable of dramatically influencing the attitude and worldview of the younger population.Filmmakers, being aware of the power that narratives have over young people, construct stories that resonate with them, teaching them important lessons about life and highlighting the value of getting an education. They successfully express the significance of pursuing academic endeavors by using approaches that are based on delivering interesting stories. Teenagers who see movies that highlight the transformational benefits of education are led to recognize the concrete and inherent significance of education, an awakening that has the ability to reroute the path of their academic pursuits and, eventually, their life.

3] Critical Thinking

Numerous films, spanning a wide range of genres, are equipped with the extraordinary capacity to teach meaningful lessons about life that have a profound effect on the viewer. Films of the science-fiction genre, in particular, stand out for their unique ability to educate and enlighten young audiences in a way that is both entertaining and inventive. Because of the complicated structure of these movies, viewers are frequently able to gain a more thorough knowledge of a variety of topics, which makes it simpler for people in general and students in particular to comprehend difficult subjects.

The importance of being able to visualize something cannot be over-stated in the field of education. People have an easier time seeing and conceptualizing difficult or abstract ideas when they are shown creative situations and visual depictions of such scenarios in films. This visual aid considerably improves comprehension, allowing for a more comprehensive and long-lasting understanding of the material that is being discussed. A science-fiction film's unique ability to combine factual information with imaginative storytelling makes it an ideal medium for the sort of visualization being discussed here. The viewing of a film that either implicitly or directly elucidates the subject matter at hand can be of tremendous assistance to students who are having difficulty grasping difficult scientific issues. These videos frequently convey scientific concepts, hypotheses, and observations in a manner that simplifies complicated material, making it easier to understand and more enjoyable to watch. Students are better able to internalize and recall the main components of the scientific issue at hand if they are able to watch these concepts evolve on the screen while they are being taught.In its most basic form, science-fiction films serve as a valuable and entertaining instructional resource that is supplemental in nature. They do this through utilizing the power of imagery as well as the ability to tell a tale, which bridges the gap between academic knowledge and practical comprehension. This potent mix not only makes comprehension easier, but it also piques one's interest and stimulates one's desire to learn, so turning the process of education into something that is both illuminating and fun.

Representation of social issues in films

The beginning of the cinematic voyage throughout the world was cloaked in silence. There was a period when movies were made without the accompaniment of sound since the technology necessary to do so was not available. Up until the late 1920s, when sound technology made its ground-breaking entrance into the realm of film, the first years of cinema, which lasted for nearly three decades, did not have any auditory upgrades added to them.

The phrases "film" and "movie" are frequently used synonymously in the language of cinema to refer to a moving picture that is created with the primary intention of being seen by a large number of people. The term "film," on the other hand, brings with it connotations of art and education and aspires to be more than merely entertaining. A movie's major goals are to grab its audience and keep them interested in what's going on, but in the process, it may unwittingly bring about societal awareness, conscience, commentary, or even inspire change. When a movie successfully connects with its audience on a personal level by being amusing, inspirational, and motivating, it transforms into a tool for spreading awareness. This is analogous to the way that healthy food gives not just sustenance but also critical nourishment.Films serve as a reflection of society in their respective places, capturing the essence of human institutions along with the culture and economy of such regions. Beyond the realm of entertainment, they play a significant role in the reconfiguration of society institutions while maintaining adherence to fundamental principles. Films are powerful tools that have the ability to start conversations, catalyze policy changes, and rally communities around important social concerns. They have the power to change people's particular views, present new aspects, and offer a variety of perspectives by means of frequently held tales.

Many modern movies have their beginnings in the widespread issues and preoccupations that people all around the world have in common. The development of international cinema throughout history has involved considerable amounts of study, creative endeavors, and the use of forward-thinking production methods. Filmmaking has risen to the top of the field of performing arts all over the world thanks in large part to the use of a variety of techniques that have been tried out and evaluated. Films frequently tackle important topics that might not be given sufficient airtime in other forms of media. [Case in point:] [C]ommercials.Films in India are divided into many categories according to the language they are spoken in, the location they are intended for, and the general subject matter of the film. When we say that a movie has significance, we are implying that it has an opinion on a certain topic, either overtly or covertly, and that it makes a statement about that topic. Meaning in cinema manifests as an expression, communication, impression, observation, thought, or judgment concerning anything, and it is frequently given in the form of an argument or a critique. When we talk about a movie having meaning, we imply that it helps us understand and make sense of the things that are being portrayed on screen.Within the realms of human culture, education, entertainment, and propaganda, film holds a place that is both singular and influential. Film, which had its beginnings in 1913 with the production of "Raja Harish Chandra," has developed into India's most effective medium for public communication, representing both the present and the past in various aspects of Indian society. Films have the potential to either lead or align with society, so affecting change and shedding light on storylines that have been concealed or suppressed. They have the ability to transform people's perspectives and views about the world and the people who live in it, and as a result, they frequently bring to light previously unknown problems or lobby for reform.The use of movies as a tool to advocate for social change is an efficient method that may be used to engage people and promote debates. Conflicts and difficulties that arise between groups of people who live in close quarters are the root cause of social issues, which are present in every society. The intricacy of social issues is embodied within society itself, and no nation has ever attained a level of perfection in which all of its residents are happy with their lives. Films, as a kind of collective experience, enable individuals to participate in conversations, with the goals of better comprehending and resolving societal concerns.T he impact that movies have on audiences all around the world is significant, since they may elicit a variety of feelings and kick off conversations. These exceptional films have a worldwide resonance, attracting attention and leaving an unforgettable imprint on audiences everywhere. One must have an appreciation for Indian cinema in order to have a complete understanding of current Indian culture. Indian films, although being largely a form of amusement, have played a key part in unifying different groups who are differentiated by caste, religion, and language. The development of Indian cinema has resulted in the emergence of renowned directors like as Satyajit Ray, as well as popular melodramatic genres that have crossed national lines and had an effect on places further afield than South West Asia.

Introduction of Indian Films

Indian Cinema may be dated back to the late 19th century, especially to the year 1896, when the Lumiere Brothers, who were renowned filmmakers from France, showed six soundless short films in Bombay, India. This event is considered to be the beginning of Indian Cinema. The arrival of these groundbreaking exhibits, which took place not long after the Lumiere brothers made their first cinematographic presentation in Paris, signaled the beginning of the film industry on the Indian subcontinent. When they first started working on their invention, the Lumiere brothers had no idea that it would one day capture and delight millions of people all around the world in a way that had never been seen before.

A scant seven months after their debut in France, the Lumiere brothers' films made their debut in Bombay in July 1896. This marked a key turning point in the cultural and social history of the Indian people. After that, in the year 1899, Harishchandra Sakharam Bhatwadekar made a film that depicted a wrestling bout in Bombay, and by the year 1901, he had produced the very first newsreel. Dada Saheb (Dhundiraj Govind) Phalke is credited with creating the silent masterpiece "Raja Harishchandra" in 1913. This film was based on a story from the Mahabharata and included themes of dignity, sacrifice, and heroic achievements. Dada Saheb Phalke is credited with producing the first feature film in India.Over the course of its history, Indian cinema has been on a journey that has spanned a century, with feature films having contributed to the development of cinematic narrative for more than 80 years. By tackling a wide variety of social, political, and aesthetic issues through the medium of film, the film industry in India has managed to keep pace with its peers from other countries across the world. Not only has Indian film been a reflection of societal shifts, but it has also been a response to those shifts, mirroring the development of new attitudes and points of view. Heroes in Indian films have experienced transformations, and their interactions with women have also witnessed shifts, expressing a shifting picture of societal standards. This is because the heroes in these films are representative of evolving norms in Indian society.

The conventional melodramas of Indian cinema have given way in recent years to more intellectually stimulating productions that investigate fundamental problems facing current Indian society. Filmmakers are increasingly showing a desire to face societal concerns without being intimidated by business trends by embracing the position of becoming social conduits, which is an increasingly popular role for filmmakers. The motion pictures "Perzania," "Black Friday," and "Water" are all great examples of how this shift has taken place and how it has resonated with both viewers and filmmakers.Films throughout the history of Indian cinema have explored a wide variety of critical social issues, ranging from racial discrimination and religious freedom to environmental concerns and the rights of women. The history of Indian cinema displays a rich tapestry of films that have done so. Films that give social criticism have been made possible because to the work of the Indian New Wave, which is sometimes referred to as Art Cinema or Parallel Cinema. The works of notable filmmakers such as Satyajit Ray and Shyam Benegal, which have received critical acclaim at renowned international cinema festivals, played important roles in ushering in this new era.In spite of this, India's cinematic environment has changed in tandem with the country's socioeconomic development. Bollywood has become a fantasy factory because to the expansion of the middle class and greater economic growth. These films show glitzy metropolitan personalities and grapple with modern concerns. Recent films like "Dum Maro Dum," "Aarakshan," and "Singham" have addressed urgent political issues including poverty and corruption on the big screen. This trend highlights the audience's thirst for more realistic storytelling and grittier stories in Indian films.In our world that is changing at such a quick pace, movies continue to be an effective medium for questioning long-held beliefs, learning about various cultures, and raising awareness about important topics. Because of its extensive reach and impact, modern Indian film has the capacity to shine light on societal issues, inspire dialogues, and eventually contribute to the constructive social transformation. Addressing these themes through cinema becomes increasingly crucial for creating a higher quality of life and comprehending the changing dynamics of society as the globe struggles with new difficulties, some of which include globalization and social identity.

It is impossible to emphasize the value of Indian film as a powerful medium for communication, particularly in a nation like India, where the literacy rate is not as high as would be hoped. Films, along with television, are useful audiovisual tools that may help break down boundaries, enhance the impact of information being communicated, and increase the likelihood that those messages will be accepted. They have the ability to mold our ideas about ourselves and the society that we live in.

As the 20th century continued, Bollywood established itself as a significant film producer on a worldwide scale, coming in third place after the United States of America and Japan in terms of the total number of motion movies produced. It was especially important that this dramatic rise in the film business took place in a country where literacy rates were not generally high since it played a vital role. Cinema became an important method of communication because to its widespread availability and its ability to give entertainment. As a result, cinema was able to have a great amount of influence over the general population and deliver messages that included both amusement and social criticism.

As a result of economic growth, increased globalization, and technological breakthroughs, contemporary societies are faced with an ever-increasing number of new difficulties; thus, it is more important than ever before for these societies to address critical social concerns. Today's movies explore topics that were previously taboo, such as the widening gap between the affluent and the poor, the impact of social injustice on the most vulnerable members of society, and the influence of globalization on social identities. In this day and age, these important concerns have been brought to the forefront, which has posed a challenge to the established standards of society and prompted a need for a reevaluation of social values.One must recognise the breadth and complexity of contemporary Indian film, which explores a diverse range of topics and presents storylines that are relatable to an international audience. The motion pictures "Chandni Bar," "Peepli Live," "Taare Zameen Par," "3 Idiots," "Swades," "Rang De Basanti," "Hare Rama Hare Krishna," "Bombay," "Mother India," "Do Bigha Zameen," and "Prem Rog" are just a few examples of movies that have received critical acclaim and sparked conversations about important social issues.It is interesting to note that the Indian cinema business has primarily created movies that endorse family values and social ethics, despite the allegation that the industry has been accused of encouraging bad effects such as smoking and violence. In recent years, there has been a growing tendency toward the production of so-called "social movies," which target a broad audience with content that is wholesome and appropriate for families. Even in films that are ostensibly about families, the ever-shifting dynamics of the film business, which are characterized by cutthroat rivalry and shifting market trends, have made it necessary to include aspects of broad appeal. This must be done without sacrificing the underlying social message.Films that are able to successfully amuse and engage the audience while also prompting them to think critically about important societal issues occupy a unique place in our culture. Films that deal with contemporary social problems go beyond the simple goal of providing pleasure; instead, they encourage viewers to think deeply about pressing social problems and to work together to strengthen the social fabric. According to the findings of social science research and the guidance of academics at universities, it is essential that more films that deal with social concerns be produced in order to provide a better understanding of the patterns that are prevalent today.To summarize, since its infancy in the latter half of the 19th century, Indian film has gone a long way, developing into a potent instrument for societal introspection and transformation along the way. The progression of the medium from the age of silent films to the present day, which is characterized by storylines that provoke thinking, exemplifies the capacity of the media to shape points of view and contribute to a deeper comprehension of the world in which we live. As the landscape of cinema continues to shift, directors and spectators alike play an important part in the development of a society that is more informed and more conscious of its social environment. Therefore, the effect of cinema extends well beyond the realm of amusement; it is a force for the progression of society as well as constructive development.

Films and Social Issues

Films have had a long-standing relationship with social concerns, themes, messages, and drama; this relationship is intricately entwined in a land-scape of cinematic representations that is always shifting and evolving. Not only has the cinema business acted as a light that illuminates the urgent concerns of the times over the course of its history, but it has also served as a mirror to reflect a wide variety of societal issues and as a catalyst for conversations on such themes. Since the beginning of the 20th century, filmmakers have struggled with and investigated a wide range of social challenges, resulting in the production of a huge diversity of films that may be used as helpful tools for gaining an understanding of and instructing others about these current topics.

In scholarly debates, the fundamental purpose of a film, particularly a feature film, is frequently regarded as entertainment and a tool for cinemas to produce income. This is especially true of Hollywood blockbuster films. On the other hand, documentaries and other genres that are conceptually comparable are seen as instruments for spreading awareness. However, these goals are not incompatible with one another; on the contrary, they may even complement one another. For example, modern Bollywood has progressed to the point where it can now handle head-on topics that were once seen to be either too controversial or too sensitive. Nowadays, topics like abortion, anarchism, child welfare, workplace safety, union organization, and atheism are being discussed, which helps to create a broader tapestry of cinematic investigation.It is becoming increasingly difficult for scholars, reviewers, and cinema enthusiasts to really interact with each and every work as the film industry continues to expand at a rate that results in hundreds of films being made year. This brings up some very important considerations concerning what makes a picture eligible to be considered a part of the national cinema, as well as what elements have an impact on such choices. There has been a movement among filmmakers in Bollywood, where they are asserting that their films matter not only as entertainment or art, but also as significant weapons for political and social criticism. This shift has occurred during the awards season in Bollywood, which is frequently filled with self-congratulation.

Abuse, violence in the home, mental illness, and other urgent concerns are important themes that touch people from all walks of life and are thus relevant to everyone. However, in polite discourse, one often steers clear of subjects like these. Films have the potential to bridge this gap and play an important role in increasing knowledge about these topics, inspiring conversation, and pushing people to take action. The motion picture business, and notably Bollywood, is becoming more aware of the vital role it can play in resolving important issues like these.In this dynamic and ever-shifting world that we live in, where the only constant is change, the rate at which movies are produced is only expected to quicken. Because there have been so many movies made over the years, it might be difficult for up-and-coming directors to choose one that is worthy of being considered among the best. It is still an important topic whether or not well-crafted films about social issues will be able to thrive in an increasingly competitive production environment. This ecosystem includes everything from low-budget YouTube videos to expensive IMAX specials.Films have been influential agents of social transformation and powerful instruments of persuasion for more than a century. Films have been used by social movements as a tool to implement a wide variety of techniques and methods in order to push for societal change. Through the use of allegory and symbolic representation, films communicate meanings that go beyond the literal, compelling spectators to think on numerous facets of life such as the dynamics of their families, the values of their cultures, and the expectations of their societies.The impact of motion pictures extends well beyond their function as simple forms of entertainment. They provide viewers with a lasting impression, which in turn shapes how those viewers see and feel about societal and cultural issues. Films have the potential to dispel myths that have been around for a long time, educate audiences about other cultures, and give a wider political, religious, or social context. They are an effective means of generating awareness, starting dialogues, and motivating people to take action in the direction of addressing both local and global issues.The subgenre of films known as "social problem films," which are distinguished by their integration of wider societal concerns into the difficulties of individual characters, has been an important component of Bollywood's huge filmography. Bollywood is the largest film business in the world, and throughout the years it has created a wide variety of movies that explore a wide range of topics and exhibit different facets of Indian culture. These movies are known as Bollywood films. While some movies are designed to be mindless entertainment, others subvert preconceived notions and tell riveting stories that are inspired by real-life events yet take place in fictitious worlds.In spite of the fact that movies present a fictitious version of real life, films frequently serve as a model for people to use in comparing and contrasting their own experiences. This influence may sometimes lead to false expectations regarding a person's social life, which can deflect focus away from the true issues that people confront in today's society. However, thoughtful filmmakers and tales that provoke thinking stimulate a critical analysis of cultural conventions and human relationships. This provides a new viewpoint and raises social conscious ness.In conclusion, the combination of moviemaking with social activism has resulted in a dynamic environment that is always shifting. Films, both as works of art and as forms of entertainment, play an important role as significant agents of change. They do this by inciting debates, posing new challenges to established standards, and putting light on a wide variety of social concerns that contribute to the formation of our world. Films are powerful not just because of their capacity to hold an audience's attention, but also because of their potential to encourage a more profound comprehension of our society and the role that we play within it.

Film a Caractere Social

The social realism film genre is a captivating cinematic category that puts its emphasis towards tales confronting and criticizing modern societal concerns. One of the hallmarks of this type of film is the use of documentary-style filmmaking. Films that use a social realism approach strive not only to entertain without providing any intellectual substance to the viewer but rather to intellectually engage the audience. The 'lowest common denominator' type of filmmaking that is so prominent in Bollywood is deliberately resisted by these films, which instead aim for a niche clientele that is predominantly made up of persons from well-educated middle-class backgrounds who possess substantial cultural capital. Unfortunately, the majority of moviegoers tend to misunderstand these kinds of films. They walk into the theater anticipating comedic moments, violent sequences, or sexually explicit scenes that aren't present, and as a result, they are confused when none of these things occur in the picture.

Artists working in the field of social realism are not only communicators; rather, they are burdened with the obligation of diving into the social difficulties of their times, performing in-depth studies, and rebuilding the reality they live in. The representation of societal reality in such a way that the spectator walks away feeling aesthetically enlightened is one of their primary objectives.In spite of the fact that social realism should be celebrated and consumed by a vast number of people, it has difficulties in the current climate of the media industry. This is partly due to the limited distribution that is the result of the restricted production budgets that are accessible to independent filmmakers. In addition, there are not many chances for display, and those that do exist are often limited to art houses or independent cinemas. The limited production budgets that are characteristic of social realism films result in lower production values. Although this may seem like a disadvantage, analytical and specialized audiences like the immersive style that lower production values provide since it successfully conveys the gritty and grim prospects that are supposed to be conveyed by these movies.Since the beginning of film, realism has been one of the primary concerns of filmmakers. The articulation of societal issues through realistic expression has been a continuous topic of discussion in the context of Indian film. It is also uncommon for people to confuse the term "realism" with "naturalism," which is a theatrical idiom that is used to create the look of "real" circumstances. The purpose of realism is to replicate the'real' under the illusion of'reality,' which may be accomplished by constructing a cinematic story that is made up of 'interlocking shots.' These pictures interconnect to instill meaning, showing the processes of realism film through a complex'suture' system. This system weaves together diverse parts in an effortless manner to build a cohesive fabric of meaning. However, the definition of'realism' in film is contested due to the fact that many realist films are not totally 'genuine' to the world that they depict.Realist representational tactics are anchored in culture and society, and they reveal the political nature of the film's visuals through seemingly unchallenged presentations. The study of realism cinema is characterized by a focus on the naturalization and normalizing of cultural hegemony. This research delves into the ways in which consciousness and value systems are formed, and how these factors either contribute to society cohesiveness or highlight its fractures.The idea of social realism is complicated, and it cannot be simply described as a genre that shares commonalities in terms of its narrative mode and stylistic conventions. It is distinguished by certain topics, such as the lives of working-class people, a filmic presentation in a realistic style, a political leaning toward the left, and recognizably iconographic subject matter, such as industrial towns and council estates. However, the classification of a movie as a social realist work exists in a hazy region, which makes it an intriguing topic for cinema scholars, reviewers, and filmmakers.

Bollywood is able to have a large amount of influence over the people who watch its films, making Indian cinema one of the most powerful means of mass communication in the country. Certain movies have stood the test of time and managed to make an impression that goes beyond merely being entertaining. These films serve as a medium through which social experiences may be expressed, bringing light on important topics that are confronted by the nation. For example, the movie "My Brother Nikhil" bravely confronts the problem of HIV/AIDS by depicting the horrible experiences and prejudices that accompany the condition.In recent years, there has been a noticeable trend in the film business toward movies that have some sort of social message, which goes against the tried-and-true formula of commercial cinema. These movies put an emphasis on substance and provide a reflection on some of the most urgent societal issues facing India today. This trend can be seen in films such as "Rang De Basanti," "Lage Raho Munnabhai," "Swades," and "Chandni Bar," all of which concentrate on tales that are based in modern Indian culture. The ever-evolving landscape of Indian film today incorporates ground-breaking ideas that strike a chord with the public and presents thought-provoking storylines that touch a nerve with spectators.It is also notable how the theme of patriotism has developed over the history of films made in Hindi. In the past, it had more of a tendency to be jingoistic and forceful, and it lacked nuance overall. However, modern films like "Rang De Basanti" and "Lage Raho Munnabhai" give a representation of patriotism that is more authentic and understandable since they incorporate the theme of patriotism more naturally into their stories. These movies are not only entertaining, but they also function as vehicles for social criticism, which allows them to engage the audience in a manner that is significant.In conclusion, the genre of cinema known as social realism possesses an enormous potential for igniting significant conversations on topics pertaining to society. Nevertheless, it encounters challenges in the shape of constrained resources and restricted possibilities for display. In spite of these obstacles, the influence of social realism on Indian society is undeniable, as Indian filmmakers continue to test the limits of their medium and confront urgent problems via their work. The ability of films to transmit potent statements and stimulate critical thought is ever-present despite the changing environment of Indian cinema; this augurs well for the potential of cinema to continue to be thought-provoking in the years to come.

Awards for Best Film on Social Issues

The National Film Awards were first given out in 1954, which is regarded as an important turning point in the history of Indian film. Their commencement marks a significant milestone. Since 1973, the Directorate of Film Festivals of the Indian Government has been the responsible custodian of these renowned prizes, which underwent a process of gradual administrative transformation throughout the course of their history. These national awards were developed with the intention of supporting filmmakers all around the country, as well as fostering superiority and originality in activities related to movie production.

Each year, the government of India chooses a national panel consisting of highly respected experts to carefully pick the winning submission in each of a number of different categories. The national award ceremonies, which are often massive events that involve celebration and acknowledgment, take place in New Delhi, which is the nation's capital city. It is during these ceremonies that the revered President of India bestows the awards upon the deserving honorees. This adds a touch of distinction and dignity to the ceremony, which is already a very special event.Within the Non-Feature Film prizes, the 'Best Film on Social Issues' award is a noteworthy sub-category that stands out among the variety of prizes that are given out. This award category was first presented in 1997 with the purpose of recognizing outstanding motion pictures that tackled important social issues such as the abolition of dowries, the treatment of women and children, drug misuse, and the rights of the disabled. The distinguished movie titled "Silent Screams: A Village Chronicle," which was directed by the well-known director O.K. Johnny, was honored with the very first prize in this particular category.O.K. Johnny, a versatile figure recognized for his documentary filmmaking prowess and keen cinema critique in Malayalam, was the rightful recipient of the inaugural award. He was also the recipient of the award because he was the first person to get it. In addition, he has made an everlasting impression on the world of literature by penning four important volumes that investigate the cultural and cinematic history of Wayanad. The honor of the coveted Rajat Kamal (Silver Lotus) is bestowed upon the winner of the competition for the "Best Film on Social Issues." This award is considered in the same high respect as the other awards that are given out for feature films.

A new program that aims to cultivate a new generation of filmmakers who are ready to confront pressing social issues through the lens of their art has recently gotten off the ground in the modern environment of the film industry. The prestigious Ford Foundation has announced the establishment of JustFilms, a creative five-year, $50 million program committed to discovering and supporting filmmakers whose works resonate with and solve important social problems. JustFilms will identify filmmakers whose works address pressing social concerns and will assist those filmmakers. When one considers the development of Indian cinema, notable figures like as Ray and Raj Kapoor immediately come to mind. These two men were instrumental in bringing Indian films to the attention of a worldwide audience. Their works, which are best exemplified by movies like "Awaara" and "Shri 420," instilled a sense of optimism and renewal in the general populace, which was especially important in the post-Independence era, when the nation struggled with the difficulties of reestablishing itself and putting the pieces back together.In the annals of film history, names like Guru Dutt, Bimal Roy, Mehboob Khan, V. Shantaram, and Shyam Benegal will forever be associated with the pioneering spirit of filmmaking. These stalwarts have committed themselves to writing stories with a purpose, which is fueled by their unyielding belief. Not only did their films depict reality, but they also sparked vital conversations about issues that are of critical importance to society.Cinema, at its core, functions as an effective medium for shedding light on important social issues and topics that are prevalent in society. It makes it possible to have a deeper knowledge of the representations of society by putting together empirical research and autobiographical therapies that investigate common disparities. The manner in which films depict racial and gender dynamics has a significant impact on ideas concerning group identification and social stratification, playing a critical part in the process by which society constructs its world view.One of the most important concerns that has arisen as a consequence of the ongoing transformation of the film industry is the requirement to increase audience tolerance and consciousness, in particular with regard to motion pictures that deal with urgent matters. Real cinema, which acts as a real mirror of society, plays a crucial part in the functioning of a democratic society by encouraging conversation and contemplation among members of that community. This shifting environment holds out hope for a future in which movies will not only be a source of enjoyment but also a driver of social transformation and technological advancement.

Ethics in Filmmaking

Within the area of ethnographic filmmaking, some moral conundrums occur as a result of the thorough construction of cinematic representations, just as is the case with every other type of media. Film, in an odd kind of way, symbolizes a dichotomy, suggesting both immediacy and timelessness at the same time.

The ethical conundrums that arise in this industry are not only caused by the public aspect of cinema, but also by the one-of-a-kind indexical and realistic features that films possess. The visual components of a film can serve as a window into the ethical underpinnings of the filmmaking process. The viewers are able to sense the filmmaker's attitude toward the subjects of their films, regardless of whether that attitude is one of respect or contempt, compassion or cynicism, arrogance or humility. For example, a documentary reveals not only the topic of discussion but also the director of the film, providing insights into the director's intellectual and behavioral perspective through the use of framing, shot juxtaposition, voice overlay, timing of speech, and other stylistic choices that either conceal or reveal the director's authorial presence. Take the process of extensively editing an interview as one example. Does this suggest cutting someone off in the middle of their sentence, denying them the time they deserve, or purposely missing lines that might create a more comprehensive depiction of them or complicate their stance? Is it possible that you are twisting their statements in order to fit a narrative that is not in line with what they actually believe? On the other hand, when using lengthy takes in filming and editing, do the people being filmed have sufficient time to communicate their points of view, or is there a risk that they will go on and on to the point where they humiliate themselves? In a similar vein, organizing major life events in a quick montage—does this make the events seem less meaningful or possibly even 'aestheticize' them? When you juxtapose images of people who come from extremely poor origins with those who come from rich homes, are you trying to suggest exploitation between classes, or are you trying to make a statement about class-based exploitation? Even if it wasn't your intention, is it unethical to leave the door open for the possibility of such reductionist readings, and how does one judge what's fair in a situation like this? Whose interests does it serve? When wrestling with these ethical problems, it is imperative that one does not lose sight of the audience(s). Nevertheless, it is essential to keep in mind that the experience of watching something should be one that is active and engaged. Because movies are open to unanticipated interpretations, it is difficult and, one could argue, undesirable to anticipate all of the different reactions that could be elicited by the subject matter. The tricky part is navigating these ethical waters while also recognizing the inherent intricacies and nuanced differences in filmmaking and human perception. This requires a fine balance.

Filmmakers need to keep an acute awareness of their target audience(s) even when they are juggling all of these different ethical issues. Having this knowledge, however, needs to coexist with the realization that watching should be an experience that involves interaction and thoughtfulness. Because movies naturally have the ability to inspire unexpected and varied interpretations, it is impracticable and poor advice to attempt to exert perfect control over how the content is received by the audience. Films have the capability to evoke unexpected and different interpretations.To successfully navigate these ethical waters, one must not only consider the intents and implications of the filmmaker, but also the intricate interaction of social values, cultural conventions, and individual points of view. Because ethical duty goes beyond the act of production to the wider influence on society, it is vital to have a comprehensive grasp of the many audiences who will be exposed to the work and the possible interpretations that they will ascribe to it.In addition, the ethical problems that are involved in the creation of ethnographic films are intertwined with larger questions of power relations, representation, and social justice. How can filmmakers responsibly utilize their influence, ensuring that the narratives they design contribute constructively to the cultural discourse rather than perpetuating negative stereotypes or reinforcing power imbalances? What are some of the ways in which filmmakers may exercise responsibility in their work?Within the confines of this ethical framework, one must also give some thought to the concept of fairness. A dedication to authenticity, truth, and a real depiction of the persons and circumstances being represented ought to be included under the umbrella of fairness as a necessary component. Acknowledging the multifaceted nature of the human experience and steering clear of narratives that are oversimplified or deceptive are both required.In conclusion, the ethics of ethnographic filmmaking are complex and multidimensional, being impacted by the filmmaking method itself, the aesthetics that come from it, the audience that it is meant for, and the wider social ramifications. Filmmakers are faced with striking a balance between their artistic expression and their ethical obligation. They must contend with conundrums that require critical analysis and an approach to narrative that is conscientious. In the end, attempting to maintain ethical standards in filmmaking is a journey that entails ongoing self-reflection, the acquisition of new knowledge, and the adjustment of one's practices in order to accommodate a society that is continuously undergoing change.

Summary

Cinematic Chronicles" is a comprehensive exploration of the intricate tapestry of the film industry and its profound impact on society. This book delves into three core dimensions of the cinematic world: film genres and styles, industry trends and innovations, and the film industry's influence on society.

In the first section, the reader embarks on a captivating journey through the diverse landscape of film genres. The book begins by defining the essence of movie genres, explaining how they function as a powerful tool to categorize and understand the world of cinema. It elaborates on some of the most prominent genres, such as comedy, drama, action, and science fiction, dissecting their unique characteristics and historical evolution. The book further investigates the art of storytelling in film, unveiling various styles of narrative that captivate audiences and breathe life into the stories told on the silver screen.

Moving into the second section, "Cinematic Chronicles" takes a closer look at the evolving film industry and its innovative technologies. It scrutinizes the role of Virtual Reality (VR) and Augmented Reality (AR) in modern filmmaking. The reader is led through the development of VR technology and its application in the creation of immersive VR films. The book addresses the challenges and complexities encountered in VR movie production, shedding light on the efforts required to merge the real and virtual worlds seamlessly. Similarly, it examines the development and influences of AR technology, with a spotlight on the groundbreaking AR film, "NEST." This section also explores the broader implications of VR and AR in the film industry, forecasting their future role and influence.

The final section of the book opens a window into the film industry's profound influence on society. It discusses the positive effects of movies on human behavior, highlighting how films can inspire, educate, and shape our perspectives. "Cinematic Chronicles" emphasizes the significant role of movies in representing and addressing pressing social issues, encouraging empathy, and sparking important conversations. The book also delves into the ethics of filmmaking, touching upon the responsibilities of film-makers and the impact of their choices on society.

Additionally, the book provides valuable insights into the globalization of the film industry, elucidating how the involvement, consumption, and production of films have transcended borders. It contemplates the future research possibilities in this domain and elucidates the various TV distribution models that have reshaped the way we consume content.

"Cinematic Chronicles: An In-Depth Journey into Film and Society" is an engaging and informative odyssey through the world of cinema. It offers readers a profound understanding of film genres, industry innovations, and the far-reaching impact of movies on society, making it a must-read for film enthusiasts, scholars, and anyone interested in the intersection of art and culture.

Conclusion

In conclusion, the realm of film genres and styles is a vast and dynamic landscape that continually evolves, shaping the way we experience and perceive cinema. Understanding movie genres provides a fundamental framework for both filmmakers and audiences, offering a roadmap to anticipate the kind of narrative, emotions, and style a film might embody. The comedy genre brings laughter and joy, highlighting the lighter aspects of life and often presenting situations that entertain and amuse. On the other hand, drama delves into the complexities of human emotions, addressing serious themes and engaging viewers on a profound level. The action genre thrills with adrenaline-pumping sequences and feats of heroism, offering an exhilarating experience. Science fiction, a genre rooted in imagination and speculative ideas, transports us to futuristic worlds and explores the potential consequences of technological advancements. The art of storytelling in film is a dynamic exploration that encapsulates various styles, narrative techniques, and approaches to engage and captivate audiences. From nonlinear narratives to unreliable narrators, filmmakers experiment with different tools to convey their stories. Understanding the power of storytelling aids filmmakers in crafting compelling narratives that resonate with audiences.

Moving forward, the film industry is witnessing a revolutionary shift with the integration of Virtual Reality (VR) and Augmented Reality (AR) technologies. VR technology immerses viewers in a virtual world, enhancing the cinematic experience and presenting new challenges and opportunities for filmmakers. However, challenges such as high production costs and the need for specialized skills are obstacles that need to be addressed. Conversely, AR technology overlays digital elements onto the real world, offering a unique blend of reality and imagination in film making.Moreover, the globalization of the film industry is transforming the landscape, influencing involvement, consumption, and production on a global scale. Filmmaking has become a global collaborative effort, allowing diverse voices and cultures to contribute to the rich tapestry of storytelling. This globalization has expanded access to films from various regions, promoting cultural exchange and understanding.In considering the influence of the film industry on society, it is evident that movies possess a powerful capacity to impact human behavior positively. Films can inspire, educate, and provoke thought, fostering empathy and understanding. Additionally, films often reflect and illuminate social issues, providing a platform for dialogue and awareness.In the midst of these developments and influences, ethics in filmmaking remains a crucial aspect. Filmmakers bear the responsibility of portraying stories with integrity, accuracy, and sensitivity, ensuring that their work upholds ethical standards and respects diverse perspectives.As we navigate the ever-evolving landscape of cinema, it is imperative to appreciate the significance of film genres, emerging technologies, and the profound influence of the film industry on society. By embracing these elements and understanding their nuances, we can enrich our cinematic experiences and contribute to a more enlightened and culturally interconnected world.

Milton Keynes UK
Ingram Content Group UK Ltd.
UKHW020904201123
432908UK00020B/3144

9 798868 974748